Luisa Franchi dell'Orto

# ANCIENT ROME

## Life and Art

SCALA

# PREFACE

This book is not only a guide to the monuments of ancient Rome, but also an attempt to understand their significance and their vital role in the daily lives the inhabitants of the city during successive periods of its urban development.

Thus, ancient Latin and Greek authors who lived in Rome or stopped there for a visit and described local events, customs and habits are often called upon to speak directly from the pages of this text.

In preparing this work, the author used the authoritative Latin editions published by Teubner, Loeb and the Oxford University Press. For the English edition of the book, the Loeb Classical Library translations were used, with few exceptions, for the major writers, and the Princeton University Press edition for the *Theodosian Code (CTh)*. The *Notitia Regionum Urbis XIV (Not Reg.)* comes from the "*Acta Inst. Rom. Regni Sueciae*", III (1949), pp. 73-106. For the more unusual works, which were translated into English directly from the author's Italian versions, the source edition is given beside the quote.

It has been considered unnecessary to furnish the text with notes or compile a bibliography. Those who wish to go more deeply into any of the topics treated in this book can use the many great reference works available, in particular, the *Cambridge Ancient History*, vols. VII-IX, Cambridge U. P., 1939-1954; A.H.M. Jones, *The Later Roman Empire 284-602*, vols. I-III, Oxford U. P., 1964; R. Bianchi Bandinelli, *Rome. Le centre du pouvoir*, Paris 1969 and *Rome. La fin de l'art antique*, Paris, 1970; the relevant headings in the *Enciclopedia dell'arte antica classica e orientale*, Istituto dell'Enciclopedia Italiana, Rome, 1958-1970. Readers who desire a complete, scientifically up-to-date guide of the ancient city can turn to the excellent *Guida archeologica di Roma*, Milan, 1974, by F. Coarelli.

Rome, November 1981                                                                                                L.F.d.O.

\* \* \* \* \* \* \*

© Copyright 1982 by SCALA, Istituto Fotografico Editoriale, Firenze
Editorial director: Francesco Papafava
Editing: Daniele Casalino and Louise Rogers
Layout: Fried Rosenstock
Translation: Carol Wasserman
Produced by SCALA
Photographs: SCALA (A. Corsini, M. Falsini, N. Grifoni, M. Sarri) with the exception of: inside front cover (ARCA, Roma); 1, 74, 100, p. 54/II (Pubbliaerfoto, Milan); p. 21/II, III, IV (Soprintendenza ai Beni Artistici e Storici, Rome); p. 49/VI (Nationalmuseum, Stockholm); 90 (B. Brizzi, Rome); p. 69/IV (Rheinischer Landesmuseum, Trier); p. 69/V, VI (Rijksmuseum van Oudheden, Leiden); p. 91/V (Alinari, Firenze)
Colour separations: Mani Fotolito, Florence
Type-setting: A-Z, Florence
Printed in Italy by KINA Italia, Milan - 2000

*Front cover: Fresco fragment showing a figure from a Bacchic scene. Rome, Antiquarium of the Palatine.*

*Inside front cover: Plan of Imperial Rome.*

*Frontispiece: A 3rd-century mosaic showing an allegory of the month of March. Opposite the statue of Mars, three cult-followers are tanning a wild boar hide. Rome, Museo Borghese.*

*Page 96: 4th-century marble inlay-work showing a tiger attacking a calf, from the Basilica of Junius Bassus. Rome, Palazzo dei Conservatori.*

*Inside back cover: Relief-model of Rome at the time of Constantine. Rome, Museo della Civiltà Romana.*

*Back cover: View of the Roman Forum.*

*1. Aerial view of the center of ancient Rome. In the foreground, to the left, is the Forum Romanum; to the right, the Palatine; above, center, the Colosseum.*

## Introduction: The Urban Development of Rome

No one knows where the name 'Rome' comes from, nor what it means. Some Greek writers (Lycophron, *Alex*. 1232 f.) connected it with the Greek word, *rhóme*, meaning strength; and there was even a legend crediting the Arcadians with first translating the original Latin name of the city, which was supposedly *Valentia* (again, meaning strength) into the Greek. On the other hand, the Romans were all of one mind in deriving the name of their city from that of its mythical founder, Romulus; although even this legend assumes different forms in different periods. The oldest version, told by the 5th century B.C. Greek historian, Hellanicus of Mytilene in Lesbos, is the one that has survived to the present day. In it, the founder of the city is Aeneas, who gives it the name of a Trojan woman, Roma. Other Greek authors speak of Rhomus, who may be Aeneas' son, or the off-spring of Ulysses and Circe. Eventually, the Alban version of the legend, with its more credible chronology, won out, and Romulus was shown to be a descendent (a very distant descendent, on his mother's side) of Aeneas' son, Ascanius.

The founding date varies too. Timaeus gives 814-13; Fabius Pictor, 748-47; Cincius Alimentus, 729-28; and the learned Roman, Varro, April 21, 754-53 B.C., a date which finally became canonical. Nevertheless, in spite of this wide variety of versions and dates, the authors all agree on one point: Romulus, with his plough, drew the sacred line which bounded his city (*Roma quadrata*) on the Palatine Hill (see Livy I, 6, 4).

The settlement was a modest one, if Tacitus' description of the boundaries is accurate in his account of the ancient *pomerium* — that is, the augural line marked by boundary stones, which encircled *Roma quadrata* and delimited the city's religious and civic jurisdiction: "From the Forum Boarium [Cattle Market] where today we see the bronze statue of a bull ... the furrow marking out the town boundary took in the great altar of Hercules. From that point, boundary-stones were interspersed at fixed intervals along the base of the

Palatine Hill up to the altar of Consus, then to the old curiae [*Curiae Veteres*], then again to the shrine of Lares, and after that to the Forum Romanum. The Forum and the Capitol, it was believed, were added to the city, not by Romulus, but by Titus Tatius" (*Ann.* XII, 24).

All the information provided in the writings of the ancients would be of only relative value to us today were it not confirmed by archaeological findings. If we exclude sporadic Bronze and Copper Age discoveries dating from the second millennium B.C., as well as traces of Apennine cultures in the St. Omobono area, we will find that the real, stable beginnings of an occupation of Roman territory occurred right on the Palatine, during the Iron Age, in the 9th century B.C. Substructures of

2. *Substructures of archaic huts on the Palatine. Post-holes and a drainage canal are cut into the tufa-stone (9th century B.C.).*

3. *Archaic cistern on the Palatine (6th century B.C.).*

4. *Reconstruction of the iron-age settlement on the Palatine. The huts had outer walls of straw and mud and, sometimes, a porch roof to shelter the entrance. Maximum hut dimensions discovered thus far: 4.90 m. x 3.60 m.*

5. *Archaic cinerary urn in the form of a hut. Rome, Antiquarium of the Forum.*

6. *Site of the ancient Forum Boarium, the round Temple of Hercules Victor (end of the 2nd century B.C.), the oldest surviving marble edifice in Rome.*

7. *Late Republic colonnade on the eastern side of the Forum Holitorium (Porticus triumphalis?).*

Introduction

6

7

*capanne* – rounded huts – have been found in front of the Magna Mater Temple and beneath the Domus Flavia. The original settlement's cemetery was below, on the site which later became the Roman Forum. Tombs containing material from Iron-Age Latin civilization have been discovered along the Via Sacra, at the Temple of Antoninus and Faustina, and at the Temple of Divus Iulius.

The city landscape in this ancient period must have consisted of a cluster of huts on the Palatine, set among wood-covered hills, with grottoes and springs where the community carried out its archaic rites (the Lupercal Cave at the Palatine, the Iuturnae Fountain in the Forum, the Cavern of Cacus on the Aventine, etc.) and, finally, at the bottom of the valley, swamplands, still crisscrossed by small streams, and frequently flooded by the Tiber. Ovid writes, "This ground, where now are the forums, was once occupied by wet swamps: a ditch was drenched with the water that overflowed from the river" (*Fasti* VI, 401 ff.).

The settlement must have been a small grouping of shepherds and farmers, but its position was advantageous; for it was right on the bend of the Tiber, where the river split encircling an island in the middle, and grew narrow enough for bridges to be built across it. It was a crossroads: Routes ran from northern Etruria to Magna Graecia at the south, and from the sea towards the mountains along the great Salt Way, the Via Salaria. It was also a market-place: At the foot of the Palatine was the Cattle Market, the Forum Boarium; and at the bottom of Capitoline Hill, the Vegetable Market, the Forum Holitorium. Here lay the wealth of Rome – in its fortunate geographical position, coupled with the coarse obstinacy and the lust for conquest of its people.

According to tradition, the first bridge over the Tiber was built by King Ancus Marcius, in the latter part of the 7th century B.C. It was made of wooden planks supported by piles, as its name indicates: Pons Sublicius, from *sublica*, meaning "a beam stuck into the earth". From this time on – but especially during the following century, when Rome was ruled by the Etruscan dynasty of Tarquin Kings – the city was alive with building activity, and it soon took on the appearance of a rich, powerful, thriving metropolis. Its area extended over all seven hills (more than 400 hectares) and was outlined by the blocks of rock outcrop composing the first Servian Walls. The later Wall of Servius, built of Grotta Oscura tufa in the 4th century B.C. (many portions are still visible today), ran nearly the same course. Its marshy valley-lands were reclaimed by means of drainage canals, including the great outfall, the Cloaca Maxima, into which all the waters flowed.

As Pliny writes, "Tarquin is said to have made tunnels large enough to allow the passage of a waggon fully loaded with hay" (*N.H.* XXXVI, xxiv, 108; cf. 105 ff.). The Temple of the Capitoline Triad rose on Capitol Hill; the Forum was paved; and, in the Murcia Valley, contests were held in the Circus Maximus, the first building designed for public entertainments.

In the centuries that followed, after the Romans had driven out the Tarquins, freed themselves of Etruscan domination, and were busy building up the political, juridical and social foundations of their Republic, starting with the publication of the Twelve Tables, laws formulated in the 5th century B.C.; and while they were also occupied in battling neighboring populations in order to enlarge their living quarters (their city), construction work in Rome continued. The Temples of Castores and Saturn in the Forum were built; and so were the Temple of Apollo and the Villa Publica in the Campus Martius, the Temple of Ceres at the foot of the Aventine Hill and, later, between the 4th and 3rd centuries B.C., the many temples of Largo Argentina (C and A), the new Servian Wall, and the Aqua Appia – the first aqueduct. The Palatine and Capitoline Hills were now thronged with temples and civic buildings, and statues adorned the public squares.

The external form of the city was definitively determined during the last two centuries of the Republic and in the Augustan Age, and its overall features remained the same throughout the life of the Empire. As Lucan was to say in later times, Rome was already the *caput mundi* (*Phars.* V, 655) and new types of buildings took their place beside the temples and promenades, theatres and circuses, baths and basilicas which crowded the

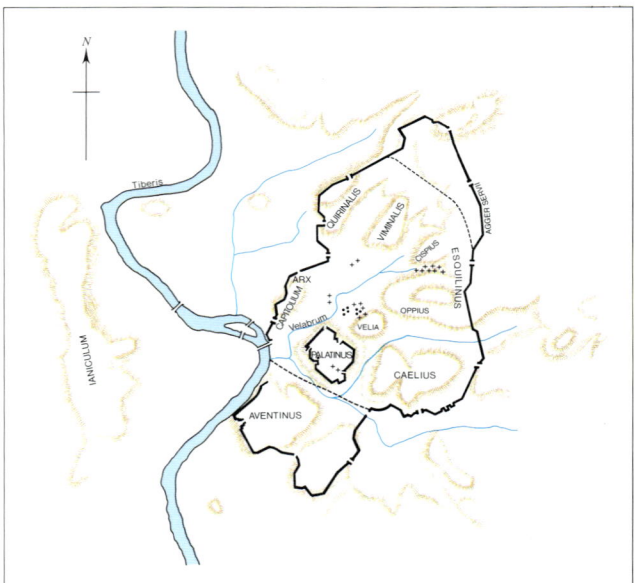

8, 9. *The Pons Milvius, Rome's oldest surviving bridge (109 B.C.), and the Pons Fabricius (62 B.C.) between the Tiber Island and the shore.*

10. *The area upon which Rome first grew. Archaic necropoleis are indicated by crosses and hut substructures by black dots.*

11. *The Servian Walls (4th century B.C.). A reconstruction of the Aventine stretch of the walls.*

12. *The Mausoleum of Augustus in the Campus Martius.*

13. *The outlet of the Cloaca Maxima, below the ancient Pons Aemilius (today's Ponte Rotto).*

14. *Augustan Rome. In 7 B.C., Augustus divided the city into 14 'regiones' or city wards and subdivided each 'regio' into 'vici', which comprised a small agglomeration of apartment buildings ('insulae'). The wards were administered by special magistrates (aediles, tribunes of the plebs, praetors) and the 'vici' by 'magistri vici' (Suetonius, Aug. XXX, 1; Dio Cassius LV, 8, 6, f.).*

# Introduction

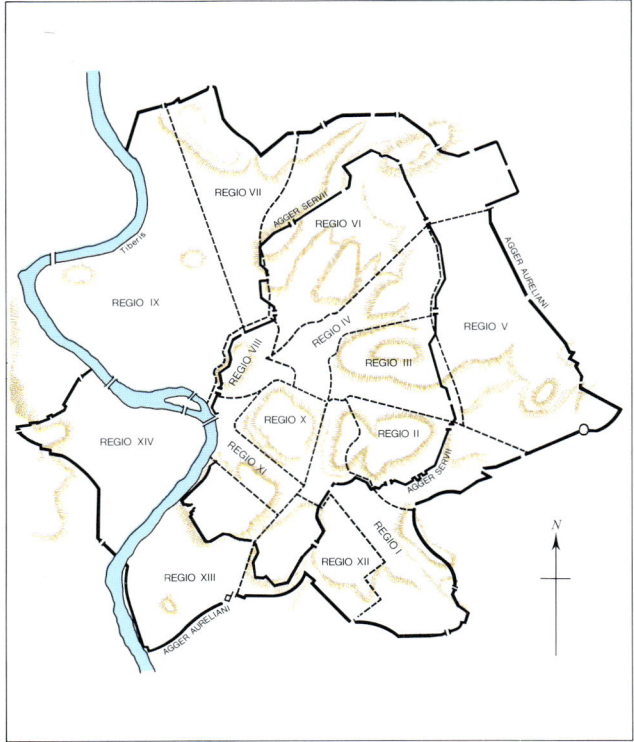

city. The enormous growth in population (there were more than half a million inhabitants in Rome at the end of the 1st century B.C.) led to the creation of gigantic commercial structures for the supply industry on the one hand (warehouses, river ports and markets) and, on the other, to the birth of crowded lower-class neighborhoods whose multi-storied, block-long tenement houses containing innumerable small living units were known as the *insulae*. The great monumental development that took place in the Forum and Capitoline Hill areas, as well as in the Campus Martius, aroused the admiration of the Greek geographer Strabo, who visited Rome many times in the years between 44 and 7 B.C., and described it thus: "Pompey, the Deified Caesar, Augustus, his sons and friends, and wife and sister, have outdone all others in their zeal for buildings and in the expense incurred. The Campus Martius contains most of these, and thus, in addition to its natural beauty, it has received still further adornment as the result of foresight. And near this campus is still another campus [probably in the area between the Pantheon and the Theatre of Marcellus], with colonnades surrounding it in very great numbers, and sacred precincts, and three theatres, and an amphitheatre, and very costly temples, in close succession to one another, giving you the impression that they are trying, as it were, to declare the rest of the city a mere accessory. For this reason, in the belief that this place was holiest of all, the Romans have erected in it the tombs of their most illustrious men and women. The most noteworthy is what is called the Mausoleum [Mausoleum of Augustus], a great mound near the river on a high foundation of white marble, thickly covered with evergreen trees to the very summit. Now on top is a bronze image of Augus-

15

16

Introduction

tus Caesar ... [and] behind the mound is a large sacred precinct with wonderful promenades ... In conclusion, on crossing the Old Forum and seeing the numerous new piazzas, lined up one after the other, and the basilicas and temples, and the Capitolium and its works of art, as well as those of the Palatium and Livia's promenade, one might well be excused for thinking that anything beyond all this exists. Such is Rome" (V, 3, 8-9).

The grandiose, monumental character of the city was increasingly accentuated by the building activities of a succession of Emperors. And then came a event – memorable for its lasting effect on the shape and appearance of the city: The great fire of 64 A.D. As Tacitus writes: "whether due to chance or to the malice of the sovereign is uncertain" (*Ann.* XV, xxxviii, 2-4 and xl, 2; cf. Suetonius, *Nero*, 38). But one thing was certain: The fire was terrible, a veritable disaster. "It took its rise in the part of the Circus touching the Palatine and Caelian Hills, where, among the shops packed with inflammable goods, the conflagration broke out, gathered strength in the same moment, and, impelled by the wind, swept the full length of the Circus ... The flames, which in full career overran the level districts first, then shot up to the heights, and sank again to harry the lower parts, kept ahead of all remedial measures, the mischief travelling fast, and the town being an easy prey owing to the narrow, twisting lanes and formless streets typical of old Rome". The fire burned for six days and six nights, and when it came to an end, only four of the city's fourteen regions "remained intact, while three were laid level with the ground. In the other seven nothing survived but a few dilapidated and half-burned shells of houses" (*Ann.* XV, xxxviii, 2-4 and xl, 2; cf. Suetonius, *Nero*, 38).

When the time for reconstruction came, however, changes were made. "In the capital ... the districts spared by the palace [expansion] were rebuilt, not, as after the Gallic fire, indiscriminately and piecemeal, but in measured lines of streets, with broad thoroughfares, buildings of restricted height, and open spaces, while colonnades were added as a protection to the front of the tenement-blocks ... Again ... there were to be no joint partitions between buildings, but each was to be surrounded by its own walls" (Tacitus, *Ann.* XV, xliii, 1). Rome had acquired its first town-plan. (see: Suetonius, *Nero*, 16, 1).

The rebirth of the city was not the work of Nero though, but of the Flavian Emperors; and lasting monuments testify to the fact: The Colos-

17

18

19

15. *Hypothetical reconstruction of the Forum Romanum in imperial times. From left to right: The Basilica Iulia, the Temple of Saturn, the Temple of Vespasian, the Temple of Concord and the Arch of Septimius Severus. In the foreground, the Rostra. At the center, in the background, the Tabularium.*

16. *The Forum Romanum, near the Tabularium.*

17, 18. *The Aurelian Walls looking towards the Porta Ardeatina and (below) the Porta Latina.*

19. *The Forum Romanum: The Rostra and the Column of Phocas.*

seum; the Baths; Titus' Arch; Domitian's Palace on the Palatine, and the Stadium he built in the Campus Martius, now Piazza Navona. During the 2nd century A.D., the growth of Rome reached its peak: It had over a million inhabitants at the century's end, and the 'Five Good Emperors', Nerva, Trajan, Hadrian, Antoninus Pius and Marcus Aurelius Antoninus, as well as the two Severi Emperors, repaired the damage wrought by other ruinous fires by adorning the city with squares and markets, baths, arches, and columns. Under Septimius Severus, a huge planimetrical map of the city engraved in marble was displayed on the enclosure wall of the restored Forum Pacis; on the part that survives today, one can still make out the holes of the clamps that held the marble slabs in place. But the Empire's power was on the wane: Aurelianus, who ruled between 271 and 275, built an enclosing wall around the immense urban area that was 6 meters high and nearly 19 kilometers long – a true bulwark of defense, and a sign of the times. After him, Diocletian also enriched the city with his enormous baths; and Maxentius built the circus on the Appian Way, and the Basilica Nova in the Forum which was completed later by Constantine. The latter decorated his monumental arch with a mixture of reliefs removed from earlier monuments, and financed the first great Christian basilicas, San Giovanni in Laterano and San Lorenzo fuori le Mura. A few more arches and several monuments were built by succeeding Emperors (the last was a column placed in the Forum in 608 A.D. by the Exarch of Italy, Smaragdus, in honor of the Byzantine Emperor, Phocas) but these late rulers excelled, above all, in the careful restoration of preexisting buildings.

From the 4th century on, new construction appeared to be a prerogative of the Church, which built innumerable basilicas – San Pietro in Vaticano, Santa Maria Maggiore, San Paolo fuori le Mura (a gift of the Emperor, Valentinian II), Santa Sabina, Santo Stefano Rotondo, Sant'Agnese, etc. –, as well as churches, oratories and *martyria*. These Christian places were often lodged in preexisting Roman buildings.

The wave of invasions of Goths and Vandals, and the consequent depopulation and impoverishment of the city; the adaptation of some ancient buildings to the Christian cult and the despoilment of others for the Popes' new construction works; and the wear and tear of time and weather began the long, slow process which gradually culminated in the ruin of ancient Rome. Between the 9th and the 12th centuries, the heart of the city (the Forum, the Capitolium and the Palatine Hill) was invaded by a forest of towers and fortresses belonging to a variety of warring noble parties. And, hemming in fortresses and towers on all sides was a veritable thicket of apartment buildings. The constant work of construction and demolition (for example, Brancaleone degli Andalò made stumps of the aristocratic towers on the site of the ancient Forum in the mid-13th century) considerably raised the ground level of the urban area; and, in the end, many ancient buildings were covered over by layers of earth and disappeared from view.

Interest in Roman antiquity was renewed with the advent of Humanism; but its nature was merely curious or scholarly, and the ruins continued to be used as stone and marble quarries for new buildings.

In 1536, Pope Paul III wrought great works of demolition in the area of the Roman Forum: Houses, churches, the remains of towers were all turned into rubble to make way for a triumphal thoroughfare leading from the Arch of Titus to the Arch of Severus, and destined to be used for Emperor Charles V's entry into Rome. When the celebration was over, the wide, empty space became a cattle pasture, the Campo Vaccino, and a huge pool-basin at the foot of the columns of the Temple of Castor and Pollux was transformed into a drinking trough. The triumphal thoroughfare, flanked by a row of elms on each side, is quite evident in Falda's 17th-century map, and for a long time it was one of the favorite promenades of Rome.

Systematic, scientific exploration of Roman antiquity began at the end of the 18th century, under the impact of Winckelmann's writings. The Swedish ambassador, C.F. von Fredenheim (1788), who uncovered the Basilica Iulia, was responsible for the earliest excavations; his work was followed at the beginning of the 19th century by that of Carlo Fea, Antonio Nibby, Pietro Rosa and Rodolfo Lanciani, and then, between the 19th and 20th centuries, by the excavations undertaken by Giacomo Boni and his successors at the head of the Ancient Monuments Board. Meanwhile, today, on the Palatine, in the Forums, and in the Campus Martius (where Augustus' great sundial has recently been discovered) men continue their labor of digging, and strive to retrieve the city of the past, hoping to improve the city of the future.

# Political Monuments

When, at the end of the 7th century B.C., Tarquinius Priscus, the Etruscan, became the fifth king of Rome, he demonstrated his will to power in a clear building programme. The small Romulean community on the Palatine had already spread to the nearby Caelian, Oppian, Esquiline, Fagutal, Cispius, Viminal and Quirinal Hills; and a first circle of walls already protected the city. The new Etruscan ruler immediately singled out the two most strategic points of the sprawling urban area: the Capitoline Hill, a veritable fortress whose steep, weathered rock walls formed a natural projecting escarpment around almost its entire perimeter; and the valley below, a natural meeting and assembly place at the foot of the surrounding plateaus. At the top of the hill, the King began construction work on a great new temple dedicated to the Capitoline Triad, Jupiter, Juno and Minerva, a temple which would supplant the Latin federal sanctuary situated on the Mons Albanus (Monte Cavo). In the valley bottom, where the Cloaca Maxima served to drain the swampland, the King (after closing the preexisting archaic cemetery located there) had the land paved for the first time, and had an open piazza created. This piazza was to bear witness to all of the most important events in the future history of Rome. It was the Roman Forum.

20. *The Tarpeian Rock on the slopes of Capitol Hill.*

21. *Reconstruction of the Capitol. In the center is the Temple of Jupiter Optimus Maximus and at the right above, near the apex of the Arce, the Temple of Giunone Moneta. Rome, Museum of Roman Civilisation.*

The political, religious and commercial center of the city of Rome was born. It contained, in the northwest corner, the Comitium, a place of public assembly; the Lapis Niger, probably a sacred enclosure dedicated to Romulus and containing a cippus with the most archaic Latin inscription; and the Shrine of Venus Cloacina, connected with the Cloaca Maxima land reclamation project. In the area to the southeast, it held the Regia, the building which housed the *Pontifex maximus* archives and the city annals; the Iuturnae Fountain; and the sanctuary of Vesta with the lodgings of her six priestesses, the Vestal Virgins. Along the two long sides of the piazza were the city merchants' wooden booths; and, at the center, the Ficus Ruminalis and the Lacus Curtius, both of them rich in legend.

With the advent of the Republic — the date traditionally given is 509 B.C. —, building activity in the Forum continued, without a break at first. New temples arose: the Temple of Saturn, in whose massive basement the *aerarium populi Romani* (the Roman State Treasury) was placed; the Temple of the Dioscuri, or Castor and Pollux, the divine twins who appeared beside the Iuturnae Fountain in the Forum at the very moment when they were seen fighting on the battlefield near Lake Regillus, at the side of the Roman army, on the day it repulsed the attack of the Tarquins and their allies in their last attempt to reconquer the city; and, near the Comitium, on the Argiletum road, the temple of Janus, whose gates were opened in times of war and closed in times of peace. The Laws of the Twelve Tables guaranteeing the nascent free institutions of Rome were published and affixed on the *rostra*, the speakers' platforms; and the Curia Hostilia was built, on the north side of the circular Comitium, to house the Senate's meetings.

All of these were modest buildings, made of tufa with a single coat of stucco. The decorations were in terracotta, and all of them were painted. The entire city had an extremely rustic appearance, which did not change much during the first three centuries of the Republic. The Romans were engaged in a series of wars which evidently absorbed all their energy. We know only of Camillus, who built the Temple of Concord at the foot of Capitol Hill when the Licinio — Sextian Laws of 367 B.C. put an end to the struggle between the patricians and the plebeians; of the prows of the ships of Antium seized in 338 B.C. and displayed on the *rostra*; and of the numerous statues of famous men put up in the Comitium.

But war brought the Romans into contact first with Magna Graecia, and later with all the great civilizations of the Hellenistic world; and the 2nd century B.C. inaugurated a period of radical change at the heart of Roman society. In the

Political Monuments

22

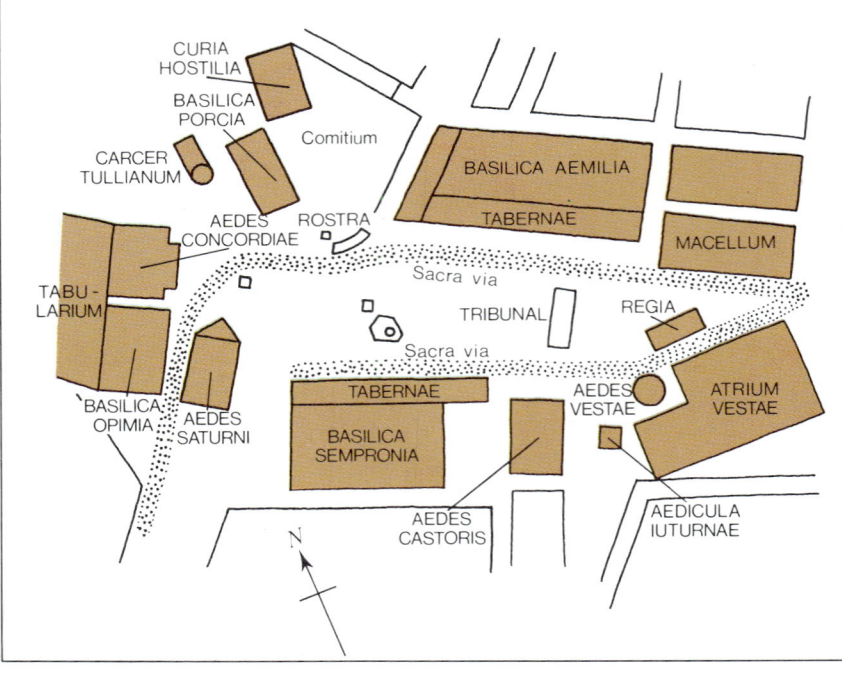

23

24

22. *Forum Romanum, circular base of the Sacellum of Venus Cloacina.*

23. *The Bocca della Verità, now preserved in the portico of the church of Santa Maria in Cosmedin. Identified by tradition as one of the ancient 'chiusini' (manholes) of the Cloaca Maxima, it portrays the face of a river god.*

Forum, the increase in wealth and the growth of the urban population was reflected in the construction of innumerable basilicas: The first basilica, the Porcia, built by Cato the Censor in 184 B.C.; the Basilica Aemilia, built in 179 B.C.; the Basilica Sempronia, in 170 B.C.; and the Opimia, in 121 B.C. The basilica was a large, rectangular edifice – a great hall which might or might not have perimetrical walls – divided into aisles by rows of columns or pillars. The central aisle was somewhat higher than the others, and had larger columns and clerestory windows. The basilica structure probably derived from similar buildings in the Greek colonies of southern Italy. In one of the short sides, or at the center of one of the long sides, it often had an apse or projecting part reserved for the tribunal – a raised platform where the magistrates sat while exercising their office. It was necessary because many citizens' activities customarily taking place outside, in the Forum, were transferred to the basilica – especially in bad weather. There were discussions about law-suits, hearings, and offices performed by a variety of magistrates; there were financial operations, commercial transactions, business interviews, and appointments involving other affairs; and there were even retailers selling their wares. All in all, the basilica was a piazza with a roof, set beside the roofless open square. And standing right in front of the new rooved basilicas were the old *tabernae* – the wooden booths of the merchants and the money changers (the *argentarii*) – which survived from earlier times and created with their presence a curious blend of old and new.

The life of the entire city was concentrated in the Forum, and all the city roads met there. Tribunes and candidates for the magistrature addressed the citizens from its many rostra; elections and political assemblies were held in its piazza; generals in triumph and processions passed it on the Via Sacra before climbing the Capitoline; great processions stopped in it for the *laudatio funebris*, the funeral oration in honor of the deceased; and sacrifices and prayers were held in it, as well as gladiatorial games, for which wooden stands were erected in front of the old *tabernae* and above them.

Human riff-raff of every imaginable sort could be found hanging about the Forum or in its vicinity, as Plautus wittily explains: "in case you wish to meet a perjurer, go to the Comitium; for a liar and a braggart, try the temple of Venus Cloacina [the Purifier]; for wealthy

Political Monuments

*24. Forum Romanum, the remains of the Regia.*

*25. Map of the Forum Romanum in Republican times.*

*26. Forum Romanum, the Temple of Vesta. Restored in accordance with the desires of Julia Domna, wife of the emperor Septimius Severus, in 191 A.D. (rebuilt and partially restored in 1930).*

*27. Forum Romanum, House of the Vestal Virgins (Severian restoration), with the three cisterns and the statues of the Senior Vestal Virgins beneath the porticoed gallery surrounding the rectangular courtyard.*

married spendthrifts, the Basilica. There too will be harlots, well-ripened ones, and men ready for a bargain, while at the Fish Market are the members of the eating clubs. In the lower forum citizens of repute and wealth stroll about; in the middle forum, near the Canal, there you find the merely showy set. Above the Lake [Lacus Curtius] are those brazen, garrulous, spiteful fellows who boldly condemn other people without reason and are open to plenty of truthful criticism themselves. Below the Old Shops [Tabernae Veteres] are those who lend and borrow upon usury. Behind the temple of Castor are those whom you would do ill to trust too quickly. In the Tuscan Quarter [Vicus Tuscus] are those men who sell themselves. In the Velabrum are the baker, the butcher, the haruspex, or any other fellow who is dedicated to vice or willing to show others the way to perdition" (Curculio, 470 ff.).

But, in reality, at that time Roman society still had simple tastes: Its custom was hard work, its nature, conservative and puritanical. Plautus' 'punks' and 'harlots' were borrowed from models in Greek New Comedy. For the moment, in Rome, such creatures kept themselves well hidden, and did not dare to appear in public often. During the wars, laws were even passed, severe laws outlawing luxury and the show of luxury. Women were forbidden to wear jewellery or expensive clothing, one's expenditures for lun-

# Building Techniques

*Opus quadratum* (dry intersecting masonry)

This method of building is the most ancient to be found in Rome (6th to 5th century B.C.). Tufa stone blocks, cut in parallelapipeds, were set without mortar in horizontal, usually alternating, rows of headers and stretchers. Ancient sources credited the Etruscans with the invention of the technique and linked its introduction into Rome with the rule of the Tarquin dynasty.

It is found in the archaic reservoirs of the Palatine, in the podium of the Temple of Jove on Capitol Hill, in the Regia edifice of the Forum and in the Servian walls.

Hoisting Systems

The dry stonework blocks and all heavy building materials were set in place with the aid of special machinery. It included *rechama* or shear legs made up of three spars set in a pyramid and a system of pulleys and claws as well as *machinae tractoriae*, huge block and tackle machinery consisting of several pulleys, each with a rope and tackle of its own. The power that set the whole apparatus in motion derived from many arms pulling all together or, when the device was furnished with sprocket wheels, the continual displacement of the weight of many slaves hanging onto the crossbars inside the wheel and making it turn.

*Opus caementicium* (concrete masonry)

This is the basic Roman system of construction, used from the end of the 3rd century B.C. to the end of the Empire. The material consisted of a mixture of mortar (generally three parts sand to one part lime) and *caementa*: That is pebbles, stone and rock chips, and fragments of travertine, marble and brick in a variable composition which depended upon the period, the available material or the desirable weight for the building under construction. The mixture, prepared beforehand in the builder's yard, was poured into a natural or artificial cavity reinforced with wooden planks when it was used for foundations; for walls it was set in wooden boxes which were later removed, or between two curtains of tufa blocks or bricks; and for vaulting it went into wooden centerings.

Concrete masonry is thus the core

I

II

that supported nearly all Roman buildings; it made possible grandiose, bold architectural achievements often in no way inferior to our modern reinforced concrete structures.

When the concrete was not cast in a facade and remained exposed, it was either plastered or stuccoed (especially the vaults).

The exposed outer-walls hiding the cement core were of various kinds, depending on period, and constitute an important element for dating monuments. The most important kinds are:

*Opus incertum* (irregular exposed stonework)

In the early days of concrete masonry, the core had no real covering facade; rather, irregularly cut blocks of stone were placed as close as possible to each other on the two exposed wall surfaces in order to form a smooth, compact exterior. This type of facade

III

*I. The Servian Walls in 'opus quadratum'.*

*II. Drum of the Mausoleum of Hadrian: The facade in 'opus caementicium' is made up of blocks of travertine, tufa and peperino. It had a marble covering.*

*III. Tracing from the tomb of the Haterii. A sprocket wheel 'machina tractoria' is visible. Vatican, Gregorian Profane Museum.*

*IV. Apse of the Temple of Venus and Rome. The 'opus caementicium' vault was built with wooden centerings.*

*V. Temple of Apollo on the Palatine. The facade is in 'opus incertum'.*

*VI. House of Livia on the Palatine. A wall in 'opus reticulatum'.*

*VII. The tombal relief of Lucius Alfius. Aquileia, Archaeological Museum. Mason's work tools: A module, a plumb-line, a compass, a set square, a plummet, a rough hewer's axe and wedges or chisels. To align the 'opus reticulatum' blocks, the mason could either use a taut rope line (colored red) or a plummet. The top of the plummet was placed against the top of the block; when the plumb-line and the hypoteneuse of the block formed a right angle, alignment was achieved.*

*VIII. Palatine, brick with stamped-in seal, set in the upper peristyle of the Domus Augustana. From the mid-1st century on, stamped-in seals, whose form varied in accordance with the period, began to appear on certain roof-tiles and bricks. The seals contained information regarding the clay quarry, the factory, the manufacturer's name, or the name of the supervisory consuls. The seals are therefore of great importance in dating all the parts of a building, whether original or the result of successive restorations.*

IV

V

VI

VII

VIII

for concrete was used in Rome from about the beginning of the 2nd to the beginning of the 1st century B.C. It is found, for instance, in the Porticus Aemilia and the Temple of Magna Mater on the Palatine.

*Opus reticulatum* (regular exposed stonework)

The coarser *opus quasi reticulatum* of the last quarter of the 2nd century B.C. preceded this facing technique, which remained in use from the beginning of the 1st century B.C. until about the middle of the 1st century A.D. It was a perfected form of the *opus incertum* and consisted of exposed blocks regularly cut into truncated pyramids and laid in straight lines set in a 45° inclined plane. As in the *opus incertum*, a wall was prepared by building up bit by bit (two or three rows at a time) the two exposed outer walls and filling them in with the cement mixture. *Opus reticulatum* can be seen in the House of the Grifi and the House of Livia on the Palatine, and in the Mausoleum of Augustus and the Auditorium of Maecenas.

*Opus testaceum* (exposed brickwork)

From the age of Julius Caesar on (especially after Tiberius) the facing par excellence of the concrete structures of Rome was formed by bricks and broken tiles. Roman manufactories always produced bricks that were square in shape, but of varying sizes: The *bipedales* had a 5.92 cm. side; the *sesquipedales* a 4.44 cm. side; and the *bessales*, a 1.97 cm. side. After baking, the bricks destined for concrete wall facing (generally the *bessales*) were either sawed or split with a pick into triangular pieces. The hypoteneuse of the triangle was laid along the wall facade, and the apex and the shorter sides wedged into the mortar of the concrete structure.

*Opus testaceum* buildings included the imperial palaces on the Palatine, the great *thermae*, the Trajan markets, barracks, temples, sepulchral monuments and the Aurelian Walls.

*Opus vittatum* (exposed stripwork)

During the rule of Constantine a mixed facing appeared, and it continued to be present throughout the 4th century. *Opus vittatum*, in which horizontal bands of brickwork alternate with horizontal rows of tufa stone, is found in the Circus of Maxentius and in the Tomb of Romulus.

*28. Forum Romanum, the small Temple of Juturna (age of Trajan) standing beside the Fountain of the same name.*

*29. Bust of Scipio Africanus. Rome, Capitoline Museum.*

*30. Forum Romanum, a view of the columns of the Temple of Saturn from the Tabularium.*

ches and dinners were limited, betting was prohibited, and expensive gifts for the end-of-the-year Saturnalia celebrations were banned. What is more, lawyers were strictly debarred from asking fees of their clients — although, of course, gifts were allowed!

With the 2nd century, prosperity returned: Carthage was subdued, Macedonia and Syria conquered, the dominions of the Iberian Peninsula extended as far as Lusitania, and the whole of Cisalpine Gaul definitively pacified, while the spoils of war fattened the State Treasury chests. Obviously, the wars brought a disproportionate share of wealth to the older landed aristocracy, which held political power; but a middle class, composed of cavalrymen (the *equites*) also began to grow. It was the first capitalist class in history, for its wealth consisted not in land, but in money, the accumulated profits of commerce and public contracts. The State did not have a bureaucratic structure capable of managing the newly-enlarged Empire and allocated contracts for almost everything, from tax-collecting to mining, from port and river toll-houses to public works of all sorts — housing, bridges, roads, ports. During this period, the Censors not only built basilicas, porticoes and temples — the Magna Mater on the Palatine; the Temples of Apollo, Iuppiter Stator and Iuno Regina in the Campus Martius; and the Temple of Faunus on

# Political Monuments

*31. Forum Romanum, the ruins of the Basilica Aemilia seen from the Curia. Three rows of marble columns divide the interior (approximately 70 x 29 m.) into four aisles.*

*32. Forum Romanum, freize from the Basilica Aemilia depicting the origins of Rome.*

*33. Forum Romanum, the ruins of the Basilica Aemilia and the square of the Forum seen from the Curia.*

the The Tiber Island, to name but a few; they also began to pave the city streets with stone, instead of the usual layer of river-gravel. Around the middle of the century, the more noble travertine made its appearance in building works alongside the volcanic tufa of olden times; and shortly before the days of the Gracchi, a new invention was made: *opus caementicium*, concrete masonry, the element that revolutionized Roman architecture, and became its most typical feature (see: *Building Techniques*, p. 14). This new technique made it possible to build structures so grandiose and bold that, were it not for the enormous transformations wrought in modern architecture by reinforced concrete, it would be absolutely unparalleled.

Although it changed slowly, very slowly (thanks to the deeply-rooted conservatism of the ruling class, of which Cato the Censor was a typical representative) life in Rome did change. In the exclusive circle of the twenty or thirty families that really counted, an interest in art and letters and the desire for a more refined and sumptuous way of life emerged.

Even among the lower classes of the urban population, there were appreciable changes. The expansion of the landed estates and the influx of large numbers of slaves into Rome (the outcome of the wars of conquest) economically damaged free labour and drove the newly unemployed small artisan and farmer classes to the city, to form the disinherited, idle urban proletariat which, from then on, would be a constant feature of Rome. The Gracchi became aware of these problems, at the cost of their lives. In 121 B.C., after the bloodbath climaxing in the massacre of Gaius Gracchus and three thousand of his supporters, the Optimates, represented by the consul, Lucius Opimius, made it their business to underline the fact that law and order and their authority had been restored, by restoring and enlarging the Temple of Concordia behind the Comitium, on the Forum outskirts. Plutarch describes the Roman reaction: "However, what vexed the people more than ... anything else was

34. *Bust of Sulla. Venice, Archaeological Museum.*

35. *The slopes of Capitol Hill: Two of the gigantic arcades of the Tabularium, the Roman state archives (78 B.C.).*

the erection of a temple of Concord by Opimius; for it was felt that he was priding himself in a manner celebrating a triumph, in view of all this slaughter of citizens. Therefore, at night, beneath the inscription on the temple, somebody carved this verse: 'A work of mad discord produces a temple of Concord'" (C. Gracchus, XVII, 6).

The great mental capacity of the citizens of ancient Rome with regard to the interpretation of the building programmes established by the political authorities cannot be sufficiently emphasized. In a society in which the tools of propaganda as we know them today (newspapers, radio, television) did not exist; in which politics was managed by a limited number of groups holding power, a number which became increasingly restricted as the era of the principate drew near; in such a society political persuasion, the diffusion of given ideas, pressure brought to bear on the population, the assertion of power and the affirmation of will were not left only to the rhetorical capacities of magistrates and generals. Other, less transitory means were also used, means which were incarnated in objects that stood before the eyes of the people day by day — in the monuments erected in the most popular public places, with their language of position, their language of layout, the precise iconography of their sculptural decorations; in the many epigraphical engravings which covered them; and in the coins which the government minted as well. The citizen of ancient times was accustomed to read in these objects meanings that are not so easily and quickly perceived by modern-day readers; to reach those meanings now, long, tiring, difficult reconstructions are often required.

The imposing facade of the Tabularium, for example, with its massive substructure of tufa blocks and its great, high arches looking down upon the Forum reminded the Romans that, around 78 B.C., after the clashes with the Italians and the bloody civil war between Marius' and Sulla's armies, the reins of power were once again solidly back in the hands of the Senate nobility.

The building programme designed by Caesar, and pursued and expanded by his successor, Augustus, was more highly articulated and subtle. Certainly, Caesar must have known that his dictatorship

Political Monuments

meant the end of Republican institutions; but he also must have known how much these institutions meant to the Romans, and how strong were their ties to the places traditionally set aside for the exercise of political office – the Comitium; the Curia Hostilia or Senate House; and the Roman Forum itself. Those very places were, in fact, the main focus of his new building plans. The speakers' rostra were moved from the Comitium to the center of the short, north side of the Forum; the old Curia Hostilia was demolished, and a new, larger one, the Curia Iulia – the Senate House visible today, although in its later, Diocletian version – was built in the corner near the Argiletum. Caesar thus restricted the Comitium area and caused it to lose its long-standing appearance as an independent space. In the Forum, where the Basilica Sempronia and the old wooden booths – the *tabernae veteres* – stood, construction work was begun on the Basilica Iulia which, as it is today, is also a work of Diocletian restoration. Caesar had taken over the most strategic points of the political heart of the city; but he did not stop at that. Beside the old Forum, he created an even more magnificent new one, with porticoes running all around it, in the Hellenistic manner; and, in the background, he built the Temple of Venus Genetrix, dedicated to the divine ancestor of his family *gens Iulia*: From Iulus son of Aeneas, who was born of the union of Venus and Anchises. This temple fixed the seal of divinity upon a power conquered by the

*36. The slopes of Capitol Hill: The columns of the Porticus Deorum Consentium.*

*37. The pavement of the Clivus Capitolinus, the 'tabernae' (shops) and the Porticus Deorum Consentium.*

*38. Bust of Cicero. Florence, the Uffizi.*

## Monument Maintenance

Augustus was the ruler who, after 11 B.C., for the first time entrusted maintenance of the city's monuments to two 'curators', the *curatores aedium sacrarum et operum locorumque publicorum p.R.*, or curators of sacred buildings and public works, praetors or consuls in rank. The lion's share of expenses for both restoration and new works was borne by the Emperor himself, with co-participation from the senate strong-box containing funds for building maintenance, funds aimed at keeping Roman property in good condition.

In about 15 A.D., after a terrible flood, Tiberius established a corps of five 'curators' of the riverbanks and riverbed (the *curatores riparum et alvei Tiberis*) whose function was to supervise the Tiber embankments and the drainage works built along its city course to ensure good navigating conditions, as well as to oversee the maintenance of the city sewage system.

There was also a corps of road magistrates, the *curatores viarum*, in existence since Augustus' time. They were praetor-rank Senators, responsible for the great consular roads as well as for street cleaning, garbage disposal and urban traffic — for example, they administered the laws prohibiting heavy vehicle transit in the city streets during the daytime.

With each new Emperor, Rome's collection of monuments grew. Suetonius tells that Domitian "erected so many and such large vaulted passageways and arches in the various regions of the city, adorned with chariots and triumphal emblems, that on one of them someone wrote in Greek: 'It is enough'" (Suetonius, *Domitian* 13, 2). By the time of the Late Empire, the city was well over-crowded with public buildings and merely ornamental structures. There were the great Aurelian Walls, the arches of aqueducts, bridges, granaries, baths, circuses, theatres and amphitheatres, temples, basilicas, squares, monumental arches, and a veritable forest of columns and commemorative statues. Consequently, the number of magistrates assigned to their maintenance had to be increased. There was a 'commissioner' of public works, the *curator operum publicorum* or *maximorum*; a curator assigned exclusively to statues, the *curator statuarum*; a 'superintendency' of the fine arts, the *tribunus rerum nitentium*; and an official

1

city architect — a very important functionary, who was in charge of city planning and new projects.

The manpower for restoration work and new building projects was supplied by masons' corporations (Symmachus, *Rel.* 14); and the material, by corporations of lime-yard workers and cart-drivers, the *calcis coctores* and *vectuarii*.

A piece of information supplied by Cassiodorus (*Var.* I, 25) is sufficient to give us an idea of the maintenance activity revolving around Rome's public buildings. He writes that funds were allocated for the manufacture of 25,000 bricks per annum, destined for use in constant repair work on Licinius, a Tiber port.

Today, devastating, irreversible degradation is the fate of these invaluable monuments — that is, of those parts of them which have survived the wear and tear of so many centuries. Air pollution, caused by combustion residues originating in automobiles and heating systems and by dust which engines of all types emit, attacks the marbles and the ancient stones and makes them crumble; it transforms them into a fine powder ready for the rains to wash away. And vibrations, the result of the transit of thousands of vehicles, daily undermine the stability of these ancient monuments.

In Rome, the automobile to population ratio is nearly one to two. One million one hundred thousand automobiles, and three hundred thousand vehicles for the transportation of merchandise circulate in the streets of the city.

*I. Pantheon interior. Built by Agrippa between 27 and 25 B.C., restored by Domitian after the fire of 80 A.D., the present-day edifice is a Hadrianic reconstruction (118-125 A.D.).*

*II. Detail of the Column of Marcus Aurelius. Today, many of the reliefs are undecipherable.*

*III. Detail of the Arch of Septimius Severus. The entablatures are slowly disappearing.*

*IV. Detail of Trajan's Column. Air pollution effects on the sculptures: A head crumbles.*

*V. Ripa Marmorata, Trajan-age Tiber embankments in the Testaccio quarter.*

*II*

*III*

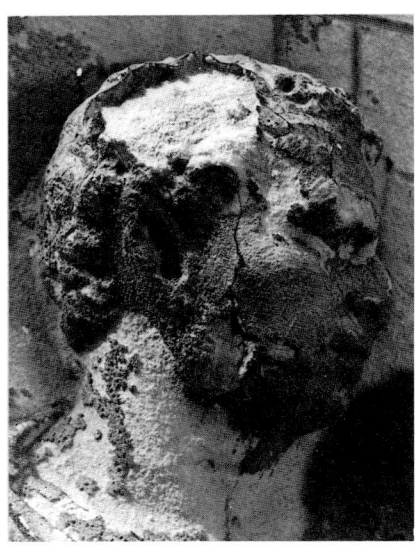

*IV*

*V*

sword, and it did so in the setting of a new Forum, the seat of a new political order.

Augustus no longer needed to resort to so much subtle allusion; after a last bloody, fratricidal battle with Anthony, he emerged as the victorious ruler of the world, the reviver of peace and the traditional way of life, the man who would bring to earth the mythical golden age. His building programmes expressed political goals which were easy to read. He meant to legitimize the new form of government – the principate – by founding it on the restoration of the ancient Republican tradition on the one hand, and on the charismatic deeds of the *gens Iulia* on the other.

He made his first move on the short south side of the Forum, by building a temple to Caesar there. Its semicircular podium at the front embraced the spot where the dictator's body had been cremated, and between the columns at the far end of the temple cella the person of Divus Iulius appeared, his head surmounted by the Julian family star – the *sidus iulium*. Suetonius writes: "He died in the fifty-sixth year of his age, and was numbered among the gods, not only by a formal decree, but also in the conviction of the common people. For at the first of the games which his heir Augustus gave in honor of his apotheosis, a comet shone for seven successive days, rising about the eleventh hour, and was believed to be the soul of Caesar, who had been taken to heaven; and this is why a star is set upon the crown of his statue's head." (*Div. Iul.* LXXXVIII). Augustus also had the Forum repaved in travertine; he completed the five-aisled Basilica Iulia and the Curia Iulia.

With the transformation of the Roman Forum into the celebrative site of the triumph and divine origins of the *gens Iulia*, access to its premises was reserved only to persons appropriately dressed. Suetonius writes that Augustus "also wanted to revive the ancient fashion of dress, and once when he saw in an assembly a throng of

39. *Forum Romanum, the Rostra, the tribunes from which orators addressed the assembled populace.*

40. *Forum Romanum, the Curia Iulia after Diocletian's reconstruction (following the fire of 283 A.D.).*

41. *Bust of Caesar. Vatican, Pio-Clementine Museum.*

Political Monuments 23

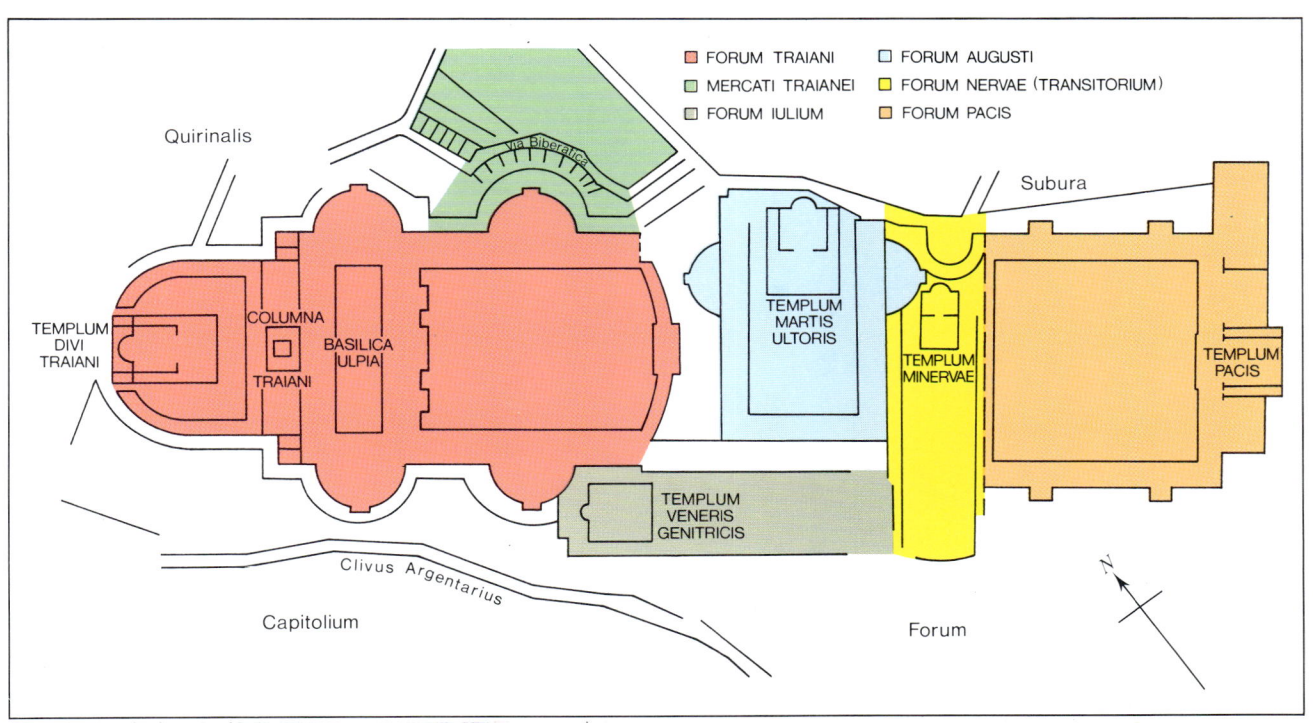

42. Plan of the Imperial Forums.

43. Forum Caesaris, south-west side. The shops ('tabernae') are visible behind the columns of the double-colonnade.

men in dark cloaks, he cried out, 'Behold them, Romans, lords of the world, the nation clad in the toga', and he directed the *aediles* never again to allow anyone in the Forum or its neighborhood except in the toga and without cloaks" (*Div. Aug.* XL, 5).

Augustus too (like Caesar) built another Forum, even larger and more spectacular than its predecessors. Doubtless it also fulfilled a real need, in a city whose population increased day by day.

Augustus' Forum had two porticoes with large exedrae on its long sides and, at its far boundary, the Temple of Mars Ultor, which was backed up against a huge dry stone wall separating it from the Roman district that lay behind – Subura, one of the most heavily populated lower class neighborhoods of the city. At the end of the portico to the left, in a huge square hall, was the colossus of Augustus; the two exedrae contained statues of Aeneas and the Kings of Alba Longa on the one side, and on the other those of Romulus and the illustrious men of the Republic. Beside the statue of Mars in the temple were statues of Venus and Divus Iulius; in the center of the square was the triumphal quadriga with Augustus.

The meaning of the iconographical scheme was unmistakable: The triumphant prince had at his side mythical, divine ancestors and men connected with the ancient Republican tradition. It was the Augustan compromise.

In another part of the city, in the Campus Martius, the Emperor's work of peace was celebrated in the Ara Pacis. Here too, in the external part of the precinct wall, the *gens Iulia* foundation legends reappeared, with Aeneas, Mars and the She-wolf suckling the twins on one side, and the symbolic figures of Roma and Tellus on the other. On the interior of the Ara Pacis, the Imperial family marched by in procession. As Suetonius wrote in his famous eulogy of Augustus' building activities: "Since the city was not adorned as the dignity of the empire demanded, and was exposed to flood and fire, he so beautified it that he could justly boast that he had found it built of brick and left it in marble" (*Div. Aug.* XXVIII, 3).

Augustus' successors erected monuments whose political message could be grasped with equal ease. Tiberius confirmed the Augustan line of peace and harmony by restoring the Temple of Castor and Pollux and Opimius' Temple of Concord. The latter became an art gallery of sorts, for in its halls sculptures and paintings by the most famous Greek artists were collected and kept on public exhibition. But the Temple of Concord was not the only 'museum' in the

*44. Forum Romanum, Temple of Divus Iulius, the cement remains of the podium.*

*45. Forum Romanum, Temple of Divus Iulius. Reconstruction sketch by O. Bronk and O. Richter.*

*46. Forum Romanum, the base of the Temple of Divus Iulius looking towards the colonnade of the Temple of Antoninus and Faustina.*

*47. Forum Romanum, the square of the Forum towards the Temple of Divus Iulius.*

Political Monuments

capital city of the Empire. Works of art could also be seen and admired in other temples (Venus Genetrix in the Forum Caesaris, Mars in the Forum Augusti, Apollo Sosianus and the Temple of Peace) and in the porticoes of Pompey, Octavia and Philip.

The most politically meaningful monuments were always crowded into the old Forum or set in its vicinity. They included Titus' Arch, celebrating the triumph over Palestine; the Arch of Septimius Severus, who vanquished the Parthians; the Temples of Divus Vespasianus and of the deified couple, Antoninus and Faustina; the Hadrian age Temple of Venus and Roma high up on Velian Ridge, still a significant pair, in spite of the fact that the last descendents of the *gens Iulia* were long since dead; and, at the center of the old piazza which by then was nothing more than a sumptuous frame for *dominus et deus* (Domitian's bold self-definition) the Emperor's eque-

48. *Forum Romanum, in the foreground the three columns and the base of the Temple of Castor and Pollux, followed by the ruins of the Basilica Iulia.*

49. *Reconstruction of the interior of the Basilica Iulia (R. Gatteschi). The building measured 49 x 101 m. and was divided into five aisles.*

50. *Forum Romanum, the columns of the Temple of Castor and Pollux.*

# Law and Order

Anyone who remembers Cicero's work will surely remember his utter amazement at the almost total lack of public systems designed to guarantee order in Republican Rome. If there had been a Roman police force, Clodius could not have acted undisturbed, and no one need have feared Cataline and his band of conspirators.

In fact, in Cicero's day the city's security was entrusted to a handful of slaves under the magistrates' command and, occasionally, to a select corps of troops composed of young men of the upper classes and placed at the service of the consuls when they were in Rome.

Augustus was the first ruler to give due consideration to the problem of order; and, at his death, he had solved it so well that it would be difficult to find the equal of his police force, even in modern cities.

Praetorian Guard (*Cohortes praetoriae*)

The corps of Praetorians, which later played such a great role in the history of Imperial Rome, was first created by Augustus to protect the person of the prince. The permanent guard consisted of nine cohorts of 1,000 men each, three billeted in Rome and six in the principal towns of Italy, where they were charged with the enforcement of law and order.

Tiberius recalled all the cohorts to Rome, where he built a great barracks for them, the Castra Praetoria. Claudius and Nero raised their number from nine to twelve and Vitellius increased it to sixteen; but Vespasian reverted to the original nine. The Corps was abolished by Constantine, because the Praetorians had strongly supported Maxentius in the battle of Milvian Bridge (312 A.D.).

Two prefects of equestrian rank, often of humble birth, commanded the Guard; although, occasionally, one man held the office – like Sejanus, sole prefect of Nero's Praetorians. The individual cohorts were headed by tribunes. Three hundred élite officials (*principales*) formed the corps of *speculatores*, whose special function was to protect the emperor and his family.

Complementing the infantrymen of the Praetorian Guard were the mounted squadrons of the *Equites Singulares*. They were not kept in active service, unless a member of the royal family personally directed military operations. Their term was 16 years; their pay, 32 *asses* (2 *denarii*); and their bonus at discharge, 5,000 *denarii*. This was preferential treatment in comparison with that of the legionaries, who had to serve twenty years or more, and received only 10 *asses* a day in pay and a final bonus of a mere 3,000 *denarii*; and who obviously looked upon their town brethren with a jaundiced eye: "the whole trade of war was comfortless and profitless: ten *asses* a day was the assessment of body and soul: with that they had to buy clothes, weapons and tents, bribe the bullying centurions and purchase a respite from duty! But whip-cut and sword-cut, stern winter and harassed summer... these, God knew, were always with them... Or did the praetorian cohorts, who had received two *denarii* a day — who were restored to hearth and home on the expiry of sixteen years — risk more danger? They did not disparage sentinal duty at Rome; still their own lot was cast among savage clans, with the enemy visible from their very tents" (Tacitus, *Annals* I, xvii, 4).

City Police (*Cohortes urbanae*)

During the civil wars, "Augustus placed Cilnius Maecenas of the equestrian order at the head of all affairs in Rome and Italy. Then, upon his advent to power, as the population was large and legal remedies dilatory, he took from the body of ex-consuls an official to coerce the slaves as well as that class of the free-born community whose boldness renders it turbulent, unless it is overawed by force" (Tacitus, *Annals* VI, xi, 2 f.). The ex-consular official appointed by Augustus after his advent to power was the *praefectus urbi* (the city prefect) which he placed at the head of three urban cohorts (later four), each with a tribune commanding it. The duties of these cohorts were above all city police duties. Although they were stationed in the city for long periods of time, they were not exonerated from active service. Their term was twenty years; their pay, lower than that of the Praetorian Guards.

Fire brigade (*Cohortes vigilum*)

During the Republican era, the task of protecting the city from fire was assigned to a small number of public slaves under one of the *aediles* and the *triumviri capitales* or *nocturni*. In 6 A.D., after a number of conflagrations, Augustus created a corps of 7,000 *Vigiles*, organized in 7 cohorts of 100 men each, placed under the unified command of a Prefect — the *praefectus vigilum*, who was second in authority only to the Praetorian prefect.

German Guard Corps (*Collegium Germanorum*)

From the days of Augustus to the days of Galba, this Guard Corps was closely connected with the Emperor. Its recruits came from tribes at the northern frontiers of the Empire: The Frisii, the Ubii, and especially the Batavi. They were not Roman citizens; they had a cemetery of their own, from which several ancient inscriptions have survived.

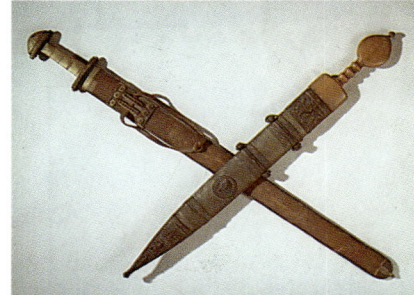

I. Domitian-age reliefs from the Chancellery Palace, detail. Vatican, Gregororian Profane Museum. The four Praetorians wear the tunic and the 'paenula', a round, sleeveless cloak with a hole for the head and, often, a hood. All are armed with shields; the first has a lance, and the others the 'pilum', the Roman infantryman's javelin.

II. Base of the Column of Antoninus Pius. The Vatican Museums. The 'Equites singulares' and the Praetorian guards bearing standards marched in parade three times around the spot on which the emperor's funeral pyre ('ustrinum') was consummated. The two parades appear simultaneously in the relief, but in reality they succeeded one another.

III. Excubitorium, guard corps of the VIIth Cohort of the 'Vigiles' in Trastevere. Another Vigiles barracks stood on the Caelian Hill, near Santa Maria in Domnica; and a Severian cavalrymen's barracks (Castra Nova Equitum Singularium) stood below San Giovanni in Laterano.

IV. Two examples of the Roman sword. Rome, Museum of Roman Civilisation.

*51. The statue of Augustus, portrayed as the 'Pontifex Maximus'. Rome, Borghese Museum.*

*52. Forum Romanum, the Augustan pavement attributed to the praetor L. Naevius Surdinus.*

*53. Reconstruction sketch of the Forum Romanum in the Augustan age (O. Bronk). From left to right: The Basilica Iulia, the Temple of Saturn, the Tabularium, the Temple of Concord and, below, the Rostra.*

strian monument, of which only the base remains. The base was reused by Trajan for a sculptural group celebrating the institution of *alimentatio Italiae*, a law allocating funds to Italian cities for small agricultural loans whose interest was designated to help support poor children. Trajan's group evidences the restrained, unrhetorical style of glorification typical of an emperor mindful of social problems; and the style reappears in equal measure on the great friezed Column illustrating his Dacian campaigns.

Trajan came to power after Nerva's brief tenure, and he tended to reinforce his image as a figure capable of opposing and eliminating the memory of Domitian's crushing tyranny. His political themes appear clearly in the coins that he minted, on which Liberty, Concord, Justice and Felicity were spelled out in words and represented in symbolic figures. He is ever-present on the column, in the military operations, the religious ceremonies, the war-time negotiations; but he never appears there as a victorious general scattering the armies of his enemy and trampling them underfoot. Rather, he is shown as a leader who divides with his soldiers the hardships and privations of war; and as a general constantly in action, always master of the situation, yet compassionate towards the men that he vanquished.

Political Monuments

Nevertheless, the emperor who was apparently so averse to each and every variety of magniloquent glorification was the selfsame emperor that conceived of the most pretentious monumental complex in the valley of the ancient Forum, and even made space for it by excavating part of the plateau between the Capitol and Quirinal Hills. In fact, according to its inscription, the Column's actual purpose was to indicate the height of the hill that had been levelled. Trajan's was the largest and the last forum of Rome (300 x 185 m).

Designed by a famous architect, Apollodorus of Damascus, it measured 330 x 185 meters and was divided into three separate areas. The first was the piazza: Porticoed, with two lateral exedrae, like Augustus' square; backed by the huge market complex; and bounded at its far end by the gigantic five-aisled Basilica — its main axis measuring 170 meters — which boasted a colossal equestrian statue of the Emperor, placed right at the center. The second was the Column, which stood in a colonnaded court between the wings of two libraries, and the third, the porticoed sanctuary with the Templum Divi Traiani. The plan of the first two areas was a copy of military camp (*principia*) planning — for Trajan was a military man, and his power was founded on the legions. But another plan emerged and was far more evident to the citizen's eye. It lay in a sequence: The triumphal equestrian statue, the Column, the Temple of the Deified Emperor.

Trajan was no Augustus; and although his self-glorification may have appeared moderate in tone to learned visitors to the libraries, in the mind of the crowds that thronged the temple or came to watch the law-suit proceedings, emancipation of slaves, or commercial transactions taking place in the Forum, its message came across loud and clear.

Trajan's crowd was quite different from the crowd of Plautus' — even Augustus' — times. It passively absorbed the messages of Imperial propaganda. Political life no longer had any bite — in fact, it no longer existed. All decisions depended upon the Emperor, who was protected by contingents of armed guards stationed in the city, served by an increasingly over-abundant bureaucracy composed of members of the equestrian class and of freedmen, surrounded and counseled by men of his own choosing, and isolated

*54. Forum Augustum, the Temple of Mars Ultor.*

*55. Forum Augusti, exedra of the left-hand portico. Statues stood in the niches framed by semicolumns. In the background, to the right, a glimpse of the square hall with the base of the Colossus of Augustus.*

*56. The facade of the Pantheon, built by Agrippa, son-in-law of Augustus, in 27 B.C.*

*57. Campus Martius, Ara Pacis Augustae, the outer enclosure.*

*58. Detail from the relief of the Ara Pacis Augustae depicting the imperial procession. The last figure on the right is Agrippa, arrayed in priestly vestments.*

*59. Titus' Arch, at the top of the Via Sacra ('in sacra via summa').*

*60. Forum Romanum, the Arch of Septimius Severus.*

from the community of citizens by the shield of court ceremony which more and more made palace life resemble life in an Eastern monarchy.

The Senatorial order was in full decline. Many ancient families had been financially ruined and decimated by proscription during the civil wars, or by battles over the Imperial throne — as in the "Year of the Three Emperors" which followed Nero's assassination; and, at the time of Hadrian's reign, only about thirty remained. New senators were recruited from among the newly enriched classes of Italy and the provinces; the one requirement was that they be men devoted to Imperial power. Senate sessions (held in the Curia Iulia or, more frequently, in the temples of the new Forums) no longer had meaning. Senate speeches, like the orations made from the rostra of the ancient Forum, were mere rhetorical exercises. Even for the better spirits, nothing was left to do but to mingle with the crowd of *ardaliones* (idle gossips), as Phaedrus in his

Political Monuments

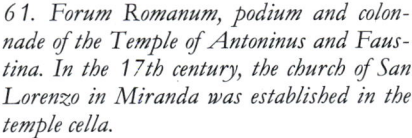

Fables (II, 5) calls the loafers wandering about in the city squares. Pliny was dismayed: "One cannot but be surprised that, take any single day in Rome, the reckoning comes out right, or at least seems to do so; and yet, if you take them in the lump, the reckoning comes out wrong. Ask anyone how he has been employed today? He will tell you, perhaps, 'I have been at the ceremony of assuming the manly robe; this friend invited me to a betrothal, this to a wedding; that desired me to attend the hearing of his cause; one begged me to be witness to his will; another called me to sit as co-assessor'. These are offices which, on the day one is engaged in them, appear necessary; yet they seem bagatelles when reckoned as your daily occupation... *Then* one is apt to reflect, How many days have I spent on trifles!" (*Ep.* I, 9). Gone are the days when a Cicero could exclaim: "Rome, my dear Rufus, Rome – stay there in that full light and *live*" (*Ad. fam.* II, xii, 2).

As for the populace, the *plebs*, from the day that Tiberius transferred to the Senate all the electoral functions that were formerly its prerogative, its political importance was on the wane. The only way that it had to make itself heard was to scream out acclamations during public ceremonies (sacrifices, military parades, etc.) or at spectacles. The custom of repeating slogans in a chorus became quite common under Constantine and after his reign. It was the *plebs* only means of expressing political opinions and making its needs known. But things were not simply left to chance: claques were organized to raise the cry of protest. And the Imperial govern-

61. *Forum Romanum, podium and colonnade of the Temple of Antoninus and Faustina. In the 17th century, the church of San Lorenzo in Miranda was established in the temple cella.*

62. *Forum Romanum, west cella of the Temple of Venus and Rome, as restored by Maxentius (307 A.D.).*

63. *Forum Nervae, southern corner of the portico, known as the 'Colonnacce'.*

# Religion and Superstition

The traditional religion of Rome, unlike the religions that we know today, concerned itself with neither morals nor metaphysics. It was essentially a set of cult practices, executed officially by a representative of the state, or privately within the family circle, and conceived of as part of the set of contractual relations between the human and the divine party, whereby the human party fulfills its obligations in the expectation that the divine party will do the same. There was no room in it for emotion or speculation. Consideration was given to only two religious sentiments: *religio*, the scruples which prevented the breaking of a vow; and *pietas*, the severity and loyalty permeating one's unswerving fulfillment of all obligations towards the divinity, as citizen and family member.

In fact, it was precisely the 'juridical' and pragmatic nature of traditional Roman religion that enabled it to maintain its hold on the community and to keep playing its role side by side with the various philosophies, beliefs and foreign cults which were increasingly introduced into Rome; until the time when it was finally supplanted by Christianity.

Originally, Roman deities were not personified. Their personification occurred after the latter part of the 3rd century B.C., when they were incorporated into the gods of the Greek Pantheon. The most highly worshipped group was the Capitoline Triad – Jove, Juno and Minerva; then came Apollo, Mars, Vesta, Venus, Hercules and the goddess Roma. In the household cult, the *Lares* were predominant. They were worshipped in the *lararium*, a small tabernacle or aedicule.

The conquest of Greece and the Eastern colonies was responsible for bringing the philosophies and cults of the Hellenistic world to Rome: Stoicism, Epicureanism and Neoplatonism for the educated classes; the Dionysian, Eleusinian and Orphic mysteries and the cults of Cybele, Isis, Osiris and Mithra, as well as Christianity for the masses. These religions had certain characteristics in common: Admission by initiation rites; teachings of the good and proper way to live one's life; judgment after death which ensures eternal salvation or punishment. In addition, there was a daily liturgy to be performed; and these divine services represented a bond between each individual and his fellow initiate that was as strong as the bond between the single devotee and his god.

I

Oriental philosophies and cults satisfied the need for an assured extraterrestrial life, the desire for certain revelation, and the longing for a knowledge of universals, all of which were emotions to be found even in minds whose ties with tradition were strongest. "Blessed is he who has been able to win knowledge of the causes of things, and has cut beneath his feet all fear and unyielding Fate, and the howls of hungry Acheron!" writes Virgil in the *Georgics* (II, 490 ff.).

But taking root side by side with the new religious practices were astrology and magic, as well as the faith in miracles and an elusive supernatural world. Even the educated classes were unable to escape the mesh of superstition (*superstitio*): "Dreams, terrors of magic, marvels, witches, ghosts of night, Thessalian portents – do you laugh at these?" Horace wonders (*Ep.* II, ii, 208 ff.).

The philosopher Iamblichus, at the end of the 3rd century, was capable of levitation and called up spirits; and the philosopher Maximus won the devotion of the Emperor, Julian, with his miracles – witnesses attest that he could make a statue laugh and induce a marble torch in his hand to burn (Eunapius, *Vit. Soph.* V, 2; VII, 2).

When, after the 4th century, the cult of the martyrs and martyrs' relics lent some color to the austere monotheism of the Church, Christian miracles took a place beside pagan miracles. Saint Augustine records seventy such miracles at Hippo Regius in less than two years (*De Civ. Dei* XXII, 8, 20).

*I. Statue of Minerva from Lavinium. Rome, Palace of the Conservators. It dates back to the latter half of the 3rd century B.C. and is one of the oldest representations of the goddess in Latium.*

*II. Statues of the Senior Vestal Virgins at the House of the Vestal Virgins in the Roman Forum. The Vestals constituted the only female priesthood of Rome. They kept alive the sacred fire which burned continuously in the adjacent Temple of Vesta. Their vows lasted thirty years and bound them to chastity. The most important major colleges of male priests were the College of Pontefices and the College of Augures, and the most important minor priesthoods were the Confraternities of the Fratres Arvales, the Salii, the Luperci and the Fetiales.*

*III. Graffito from the Paedagogium (3rd century A.D.) on the Palatine. It shows a caricature of the Crucifix. The inscription in Greek reads 'Alexamenos adores God'.*

*IV. Priest of Cybele. Rome, Capitoline Museum. The cult of Cybele, the Magna Mater, was introduced into Rome in 204 B.C. The priest is shown with Attis, portrayed in the medallions to the sides of his diadem and in the pendant on his breast, and he is surrounded by the musical instruments used in cult rites: Cymbals, tambourine and two flutes ('tibia' and 'keras' or curved horn).*

*V. Mithras Group. Vatican, Pio-Clementine Museum. Mithras slays the mystic bull from whose blood life flows through the entire universe. Mithraism featured great moral rigor, and was connected with Babylonian astrology. After death, Mithra assigns believers a place in hell or in heaven, divided up into seven grades which correspond to the celestial bodies. The ritual also included the consecration of bread and drink.*

*VI. Temple of Portunus in the Forum Boarium.*

II

III

IV

VI

V

*64. Forum Romanum, one of the plutei from Trajan's group celebrating the institution of 'alimentatio Italiae'. It depicts: To the left, the Emperor speaking from the Rostra of the Temple of Divus Iulius; in the background, the south side of the Forum Romanum (the Parthian Arch of Augustus, the Temple of Castor and Pollux, the opening of the Vicus Tuscus and the Basilica Iulia); to the right, the statue of Marsyas, the Ficus Ruminalis and the sculptural group with Trajan and Italia.*

*65. Trajan's Column, detail of the spiral frieze which narrates the events of the Dacian Wars.*

*66. Forum Traiani, the great north-east exedra of the square, co-axial with the exedra containing the shops of Trajan's markets.*

ment was not deaf to the voice of the people, to judge by the words of the Edict of Constantine: "Moreover, We grant to all persons the privilege of praising by public acclamation the most just and vigilant judges, so that We may grant increased accessions of honor to them. On the contrary, the unjust and the evildoers must be accused by cries of complaint, in order that the force of Our censure may destroy them" (*CTh* I, 16, 6 year 331).

Curiously enough, during the Late Empire Senators and *plebs* were united in causing the social decay of the city through their progressive loss of civic spirit. The only things that mattered to Senators, as indeed to all men of equestrian rank, were the wealth and social position (and resultant exemption from taxes) that derived from political and administrative office.

The truth is that during the reign of Septimius Severus a radical change occurred in the structure of society, from that time on, the only people that counted in Rome were bureaucrats and military men, most of them of middle-class and non-Roman origins. This new political leadership imposed on the rest of society a less refined, more provincial way of life; religious ideas in which oriental cults, including Christianity, were predominant; and an artistic culture whose inspiration lay at a great distance from Hellenistic naturalism. It first found expression in the reliefs on the arch of Septimius

Political Monuments

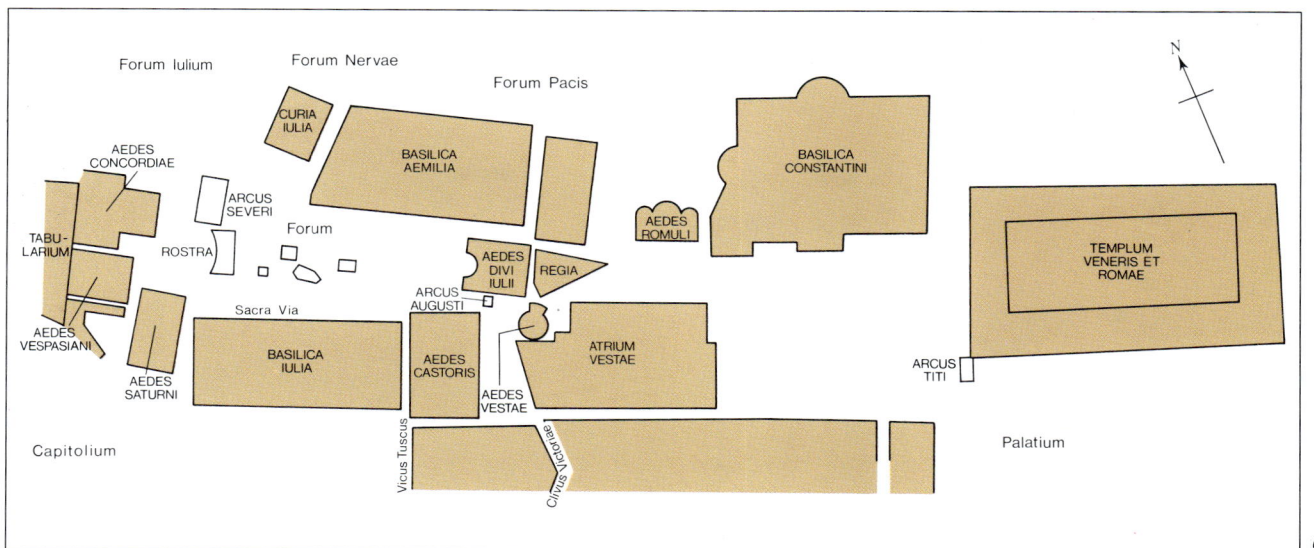

67. Plan of the Forum Romanum in the Late Empire.

68. Arch of Constantine, the Constantinian frieze, the Hadrianic tondi and the Aurelian attic reliefs.

69, 70. Forum Romanum, two sides of the base of the column erected in honor of the Decennalia of Diocletian's tetrarchy (303 A.D.). The bas-reliefs depict the Emperor's libation (above) and the sacrifice of the bull, ram and pig.

Political Monuments

Severus; and it was absolute master in the frieze of the last great political monument of Rome, the Arch of Constantine, forerunner of innumerable medieval reliefs.

Constantine's arch was built to celebrate his victory over Maxentius at the Battle of Milvian Bridge, on October 28, 312 A.D. But victory was obtained with the protection – actually, "at the instigation" – of the divinity: *instinctus divinitatis* are the words of the inscription on the attic of the arch; it was not won by the Emperor's genius (*mentis magnitudine*) alone. The monument was a pastiche of sculptures taken from preexisting structures, a serious sign of the decay of artistic craftsmanship in Rome.

Constantine's arch celebrated the victory "over tyranny and all of its following" – *de tyranno quam de omni eius factione*; but it also clearly propagated another concept, a concept which would become a cornerstone of absolute monarchy from the 3rd century until the French Revolution – the concept of the *divina maiestas* of the Emperor. In the Hadrian age *tondi*, Constantine's head, which replaced that of his distant predecessor, was encircled by the nimbus; in the frieze (in the scenes of the *oratio*: The speech, and the *liberalitas*: The distribution of allowances to the poor) the Emperor, immobile, was depicted in the frontal, hieratical pose required by court etiquette, with his figure unnaturally larger than the surrounding figures. Symbol prevailed over nature, and the Emperor showed himself to the people in his divine form.

But, while the arch was under construction, Constantine's capital was Trier, in Germany; and it was Sirmium in Illyria, and Serdica in Thrace before Constantinople was founded. Rome was no longer the throbbing heart of the Empire, and great monuments would speak no more to the "*turba Remi*" (mob of Remus), Juvenal's old invective for the Quiriti (*Sat*. X, 73; cf. Catullus, LVIII, 5) in the language of Imperial propaganda.

71. *The Column of Marcus Aurelius (180-196 A.D.).*

72. *The equestrian statue of Marcus Aurelius in the square of the Capitol.*

73. *Forum Romanum, north side of the Basilica of Maxentius. In the central hall one may glimpse the niches which held statues and the coffering of the vault ceiling.*

*74. The Circus Maximus at the foot of the Palatine. Aerial view.*

## Public Buildings

"And what does the mob of Remus say? ... Now that no one buys our votes, the public has long since cast off its cares; the people that once bestowed commands, consulships, legions and all else, now meddles no more and longs eagerly for just two things – Bread and Games [*panem et circenses*]!" (Juvenal, *Sat.* X, 72 ff.).

Food and free entertainment were a right which the urban populace acquired under the Empire. This right derived from ancient Republican customs consolidated in the days when the plebeians still had the power conferred on them by the vote; when ambitious politicians fawned on them at election time, and organized magnificent gladiatorial games and 'hunts' with wild animals for their pleasure, as well as offerings of free food (grain distributions) to soothe their hunger. At the end of the Republican era, the cost of a political career was exorbitant enough to provoke Caesar's banker Crassus' remark that "no amount of wealth was great enough for the man who aspired to be the foremost citizen of the state" (Cicero, *De Off.* I, viii, 25).

In Cicero's day, the "Roman people" had already become "the sordid dregs of the populace", "the dregs of humanity collected by Romulus", "that blood-sucker of the treasury, the wretched and starveling mob" (Cicero, *Ad Att.* I, xvi, 11; II, i, 8). The populace was a lazy multitude threatening at all times to enact its perilous transformation into innumerable, roving bands of violent agitators (as it had in Clodius' time), therefore, it had to be humored and

75. Relief from the tomb of a circus magistrate, depicting a chariot race (Age of Hadrian). Vatican, Gregorian Profane Museum.

76-79. Mosaic with horses and charioteers wearing their team colors. Rome, Museo delle Terme.

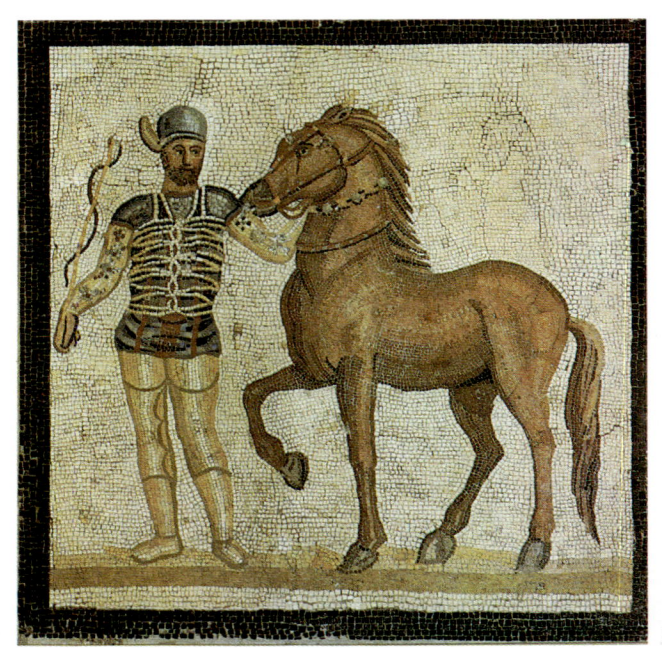

Public Buildings

80. *A Roman consul with the various 'factiones' (teams) of the circus. Marble inlay from the Basilica of Junius Bassus in Rome (330-350 A.D.). Florence, Palazzo Vecchio.*

81. *The Circus of Maxentius on the Via Appia, the central rib and the course viewed from the archway.*

82. *Circus of Maxentius on the Via Appia, the towers flanking the 'carceres'.*

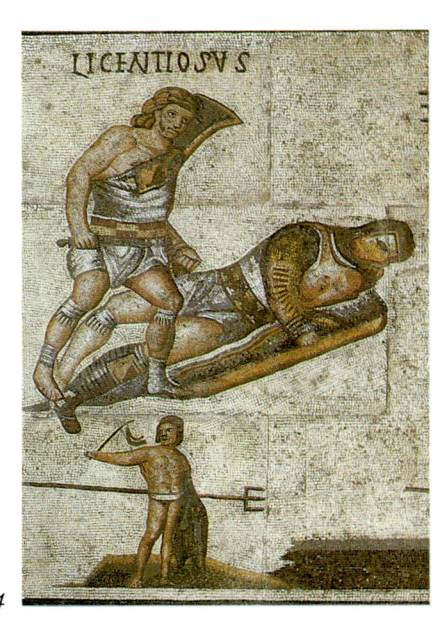

83-85. *Detail of the great mosaic from Tusculum, with gladiatorial and venatic scenes (latter half of the 3rd century A.D.). Rome, Borghese Museum.*

86. *The Ludus Magnus, near the Colosseum. Built by Domitian, it was the most important gladiatorial barracks.*

kept under control. And the reins of state subsidies and public entertainments were drawn tighter and tighter as the ranks of the urban proletariat swelled and its political prerogatives were lost.

In Nero's time, liberty for a freed slave meant anyone's right to become "the possessor of a ticket for a ration of mangy spelt" (Persius, *Sat.* V, 74 f.) and Trajan, with the wisdom of an "excellent prince", "always looked with great attention to the stars of the theatre, circus and arena; for he well knew that the measure of excellence in government lies no less in the amusements it provides than in its care for more important matters, and that although the distribution of grain and money allowances satisfies each citizen taken individually, the spectacle is necessary to make content the people as a whole" (Dio Cassius, LXVI, 10).

In today's world, a political system which tends to increase lower-class idleness without creating new urban jobs or even sending the unemployed to the country to dig up untilled land (a fairly difficult operation even when the Romans founded their colonies) may seem an inexplicable and risky politics. In truth, some Emperors, like Augustus, were aware of the risks. Nevertheless, during the whole period of Roman antiquity, this type of politics was the constant guiding principle of state management, which saw in the spectacle a new instrument of propaganda. One ought not, however, to underestimate the fact that during the Empire, gladiatorial games, circus competitions and theatrical performances were not simply 'transference' objects for the frustrations or the violent moods of populace. They were also an important part of the social routine of the Senatorial class which, by then, had also been deprived of political duties. Under Constantine and his successors, Roman senators were still obliged to organize games to celebrate the appointment of quaestor, praetor and *consul suffectus*; and the great families were bound to a tradition of lavishness which led them to spend breathtaking sum. At the end of the 4th century, Aurelius Symmachus spent 2,000 pounds of gold (65.50 kg.) for his son's praetorian games; and a century later, Petronius Maximus spent over 4,000 pounds for his own (Olympiodorus, *FHG* IV, 44). The emperors interceded many times over, attempting to curb this extravagance in the interests of the less well-to-do Senatorial families; although the latter were allowed to group together and pool their resources to meet the cost of the games, when the occasion arose (*CTh* VI, 4, 21 § 6, year 372).

Obviously, the emperors themselves vied with one another and outdistanced the magistrates when it came to offering magnificent spectacles to the people of Rome; and they added to their offerings a considerable amount of building activity, undertaken to provide the city with well-equipped establishments to house the shows.

The oldest Roman entertainment (*ludus*) was the two-, three-, or four-horse chariot race, held in the circus.

The Circus Maximus in the Murcia Valley, between the Palatine and Aventine Hills, was said to date back to the age of the Tarquins; and for a long, long, time its spectators' tribunes and its starting gates (*carceres*), from which the competing chariots burst forth at the signal to begin, remained primitive wooden structures. Claudius rebuilt them in marble; but Trajan ordered the definitive transformation of the circus. He made it a monumental structure with a total length — including arena and steps — of 600 meters, an average width of over 100 meters, and a maximum capacity of 385,000 persons.

The stairs rested upon a substructure consisting of three rows of arches built of brickwork masonry partially finished in marble. A maximum of twelve chariots could compete, and they could enter the arena simultaneously from the twelve *carceres* at the northern end of the circus. From the magistrate's tribune above the *carceres*, the president of the competition gave the starting signal by throwing a napkin — the *mappa* — into the arena. The Imperial tribune (*pulvinar*) was situated on the Palatine Hill side of the circus.

The chariots — *bigae* (two-horse), *trigae* (three-horse) and *quadrigae* (four-horse) — ran the race in a counterclockwise direction, circling round the *spina*, a high, 344-meter-long masonry rib built along the central axis of the circus and bearing statues, trophies and the seven movable marble eggs and seven dolphins serving to count the race's seven laps. At its two ends were the *metae* or turning posts, large gilded bronze cones. Later, Augustus had another object placed upon it: An Obelisk of Ramses II, brought to Rome from Egypt (now in Piazza del Popolo); and in 357 A.D. Constantine II added the Obelisk of Thutmose III (now restored in Piazza San Giovanni in Laterano).

Until the late Republican era, all the jockeys belonged to teams (*factiones*) and each team had its own colors, worn by its charioteers.

87. High relief depicting circus scenes. L'Aquila, National Museum of Abruzzo.

88. Gladiator's bronze helmet. Naples, National Archaeological Museum.

## Supplies

In the days of the Republic, the city of Rome had no municipal council, nor even any real municipal magistrates. The Senate and other magistracies were generally too absorbed by the vaster problems that beset Italy and the growing mass of provinces to do much for Rome. The responsibilities that are entrusted to specialists in modern cities were assigned by lots to the *aediles* magistrates whose term lasted only one year in Republican times. The censors occasionally handled public building administration.

Augustus was the first ruler to become aware of the need to create non-political organs for handling the practical problems of local administration, first and foremost among which was the problem of supplies.

### Grain

During the Republican era, the *aediles* often had difficulty in guaranteeing the supply of foodstuffs (especially of grain) to the urban population. Caesar created two new *aediles* specifically for this task, the *aediles ceriales*; and Augustus entrusted the job to a Prefect, the *Praefectus annonae* of equestrian rank who headed a huge department with representatives scattered throughout the ports of Italy and the provinces. Of particular importance were the Ostia offices, for food supplies poured into the port of this city from all over the Empire.

A corollary of the supply problem was the problem of supervising grain distribution to the poorer citizens, either free or at a subsidized, lower-than-market price. The practice was initiated by Gaius Gracchus, in a law of 123 B.C.; and newly regulated by Augustus, who assigned special magistrates to control it — the *praefecti frumenti dandi ex s.c.*, closely connected with the Annona Prefect. Augustus limited the number of beneficiaries to 200,000, the *plebs frumentaria*. They held ration cards, which at the beginning of the 3rd century were hereditary and saleable. By the end of the 5th century, many of these cards had passed into the hands of the Church.

From the time of Claudius on, grain distribution took place on pre-established days and in accordance with a list published beforehand in a vast, porticoed square (the *porticus Minucia frumentaria*) situated immediately to the east of the complex of temples in Largo Argentina. After Aurelianus, instead of grain, there were daily distributions of bread. The number of beneficiaries in the Late Empire was 120,000 (*CTh* XIV, 17, 2-6). They received other food subsidies as well: Oil, which was dispensed in as many as 2,300 city shops, the so-called *mensae oleariae*, in the days of Septimius Severus and thereafter (*SHA*, Sev. XVIII, 3); and pork meat, distributed, however, during only five months of the year. The meat ration (*opsonium*) was five pounds a month per beneficiary. Each day the butchers made 4,000 distributions, which went to make up the pre-established monthly total of 120,000 (*CTh* XIV, 4, 10, 3, 5).

### Water

During the Republican era, the city water-supply was supervised by the censors, while a corps of public slaves was kept for the construction of new aqueducts and for maintenance services.

At the end of the 1st century A.D., water flowed to Rome through nine aqueducts. Trajan made an addition with his aqueduct in 109, as did Alexander Severus with his, in about 226. Some aqueducts supplied only public buildings, while others carried water to reservoirs and cisterns (*lacus*) with which private consumers could be linked up. At the end of the 4th century, there were, in all, 1,352 of these reservoirs. Consumers had to obtain an imperial concession for private water supply, and tube diameter was regulated by precise laws (*CTh* XV, 2, 5, year 389; XV, 2, 3, year 382).

*I. Frieze from the tomb of Eurysaces at Porta Maggiore, showing the different stages of bread-making. At the end of the 4th century, in Rome, there were 274 bakeries involved in the production of bread for free distribution, ('panis gradilis'). The bakeries were huge establishments with slaves, and beasts of burden kept to turn the millstones. Gradually, brute force in milling was supplanted by water power, supplied from the aqueducts. The first mention of water mills appears in a law of 398 A.D. (CTh XIV, 15, 4). By the 6th century there were water mills everywhere. When the Goths besieged Rome and cut off the aqueducts in 536, all the mills were brought to a halt; and there would have been no more bread in Rome if Belisarius had not put into action his clever plan, which put the Tiber waters to use in milling (Procopius, Bell. Goth. I, 19, 19 ff.).*

*II. Dolium Warehouse at Ostia. Merchandise was stored in huge multi-storied buildings ('horrea') divided into many rooms generally laid out around a porticoed central court, and sometimes furnished with huge terracotta jars ('dolia') fitted into the pavement.*

*III. Large wine cellar. rebuilt in accordance with Palladian indications (I, 18). 1 - Pressing platform; 2 - Grape must collection basins; 3 - Miniature canals and terracotta tubes, which carried the must outside, where it was collected in 'dolia' (jars) for storage; 4 - 'Dolia'; 5 - Raised platform with floor bases for 'dolia'; 6 - The filled 'dolia' were transferred to the cellar interior (from H. Plommer).*

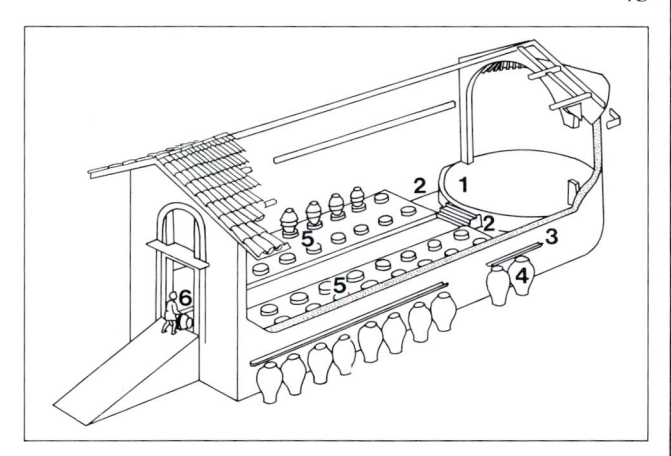

*IV. Lead water pipes. Palatine, Antiquarium. During the entire 1st century A.D., pipes ('fistulae aquariae') were customarily marked with the owner's name.*

*V. Amphora for the transport of wine from the cargo of a freighter. Albenga, Civic Museum. Aurelianus wanted to distribute free wine to the Romans too, but he was dissuaded by a praetor, who argued: "if we give wine to the people of Rome, we may as well give them chickens and geese too!" (SHA, Aurel. XLVIII, 1-3).*

*VI. Series of arcades from the Claudian Aqueduct. The first Roman aqueducts (Aqua Appia, Anio Vetus) were underground structures running along in a channel built of juxtaposed dry tufa blocks. The first elevated aqueduct was the Aqua Marcia, begun in 144 B.C.*

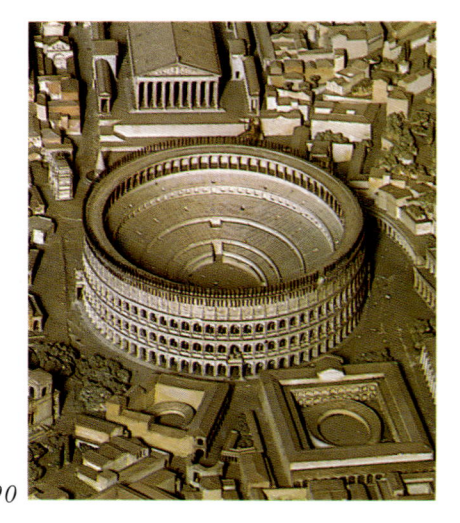

89. Colosseum, the cavea tiers and the unpaved arena. Beneath, a view of the network of corridors and service rooms.

90. Reconstruction of the Colosseum. Rome, Museum of Roman Civilisation. The Ludus Magnus and the barracks where the gladiators were trained are visible at the lower right; to the left are the Ludus Matutinus where the animal trainers practised. Both these constructions had a small auxiliary arena.

From Augustus' rule until the end of the Empire, there were almost unvaryingly four team colors: White, worn by the Albata, red by the Russata, blue by the Veneta, green by the Prassina. The *factiones* were companies or corporations; they supplied teams to the magistrates giving the games and received money prizes in return.

Popular enthusiasm during the races ran high and such competitions provided an innocuous subject for dinner gossip among friends in the days when tyrants had a thousand ears: "[Let there be] jests without gall, and a freedom not to be dreaded the next morning and no word you would wish unsaid; let my guests converse of the Green and the Blue..." (Martial, X, xlviii, 21 ff.). Betting and charming new acquaintances followed in their wake: "Such sights are for the young, whom it befits to shout and make bold wagers with a smart damsel by their side" (Juvenal, *Sat.* XI, 201 ff.). Star circus performers, charioteers and horses were idolized and well-paid: "in a single hour, Scorpus, a winner of the race bears off fifteen bags of gleaming gold" (Martial, X, lxxiv, 5 f.).

During the late Empire, the popularity of chariot racing became increasingly widespread, and its startling growth led to the supposition (unsupported by actual sources) that the *factiones* were identified with religious or political groups. Romans lined up for good seats long before dawn. Procopius was scandalized by what he saw in the 6th century. "In every city the population has been divided for a long time past into the Blue and the Green factions; but within comparatively recent times it has come about that for the sake of these names and the seats which the rival factions occupy in watching the games, they spend their money and abandon their bodies to the most cruel tortures, and do not even think it unworthy to die a most shameful death. [And] they fight against their opponents knowing not for what end they imperil themselves... So there

Public Buildings

grows up in them against their fellow men a hostility which has no cause ... [and which] gives place neither to the ties of marriage nor of relationship nor of friendship, and the case is the same even though those who differ with respect to these colours be brothers or any other kin ... Even when they are perhaps ill supplied with the necessities of life, and when their fatherland is in the most pressing need and suffering injustly, they pay no heed if only it is likely to go well with their 'faction'; for so they name the bands of partisans. And even women join with them in this unholy strife, and they not only follow the men, but even disagree with them if opportunity offers ... So that I, for my part, am unable to call this anything except a disease of the soul" (*Bell. Pers.* I, 24, 2 - 6).

But other, new circuses were built in Rome. There was the Republican era Circus Flaminius in the area near today's Via delle Botteghe Oscure. There was Caligula's private circus in the Gardens of Agrippina (now the Horti Agrippinae in the Vatican) where Nero practiced racing before his public exhibitions. There was the great Circus of Maxentius, the only Roman circus whose entire perimeter has been preserved, including the two towers flanking each of its *carceres*.

Popular enthusiasm for the circus games was fully equalled by the passion for the *munera* — gladiatorial combats held in the arena. Probably of Etruscan origin and connected with funeral ceremonies, later adopted and modified in Campania, gladiatorial exhibitions took their place among the public spectacles of Rome in 105 B.C.; and until the first amphitheatres were built (Curio's in 53 B.C., and Caesar's in 46 B.C.) they were held in the Forum, where on show days the old merchants' booths lining the long sides of the square were obscured by the wooden spectator's tribunes set up above and in front of them.

The first gladiators were prisoners-of-war condemned to death;

91. *Colosseum, cavea tier substructures.*

92. *Colosseum, ground floor gallery.*

93. *Mosaic shown in figures 83-85. Detail with venatic scene. Rome, Borghese Museum.*

94. *The Colosseum, view of the exterior collonnade.*

but among them were also free men who voluntarily engaged themselves as mercenaries. The barracks were comfortable and the food good because members of the gladiatorial corps were valuable merchandise. On the other hand, training was difficult and the discipline strict. There was an imperial gladiatorial school in Rome: The Ludus Magnus, at the Colosseum. Combat fell into several categories, identified by the way in which the gladiators were armed. There was the *Retiarius* of literary and iconographical fame, clad in a mere loin-cloth held in place by a belt, helmetless, without shin-guard, protected only by a large armlet fixed to his left shoulder with a raised wing-piece (*galerus*) which he used to shield his face: He fought with dagger, trident, and a net to entangle his adversary. The Thracian (*thraces* or *thraeces*) had a broad-brimmed helmet with a crest, a shin-guard, a protective sleeve on his right arm, and a small round or square shield, the *parmula*. He fought with a *sica*, a straight or curved short sword. We know the names of many other types of gladiator – *secutor, murmillo, provocator, saggittarius, oplomachus*, etc. –, but they are difficult to identify in those pictures available to us.

Gladiatorial combats were announced in handbills distributed along the streets (*libelli munerari*), and in huge hand-written 'posters' on the walls.

The *velarium*, an enormous cloth spread over the amphitheatre steps to protect them from the sun, was an extremely important accessory at these spectacles, which ordinarily began in the early afternoon. When the amphitheatre was equipped with one, it was inevitably mentioned in the announcements. At times *sparsiones*, water or perfume sprinkled from above to refresh the spectators, were also mentioned (*Iscrizioni pompeiane*, edited by G.O. Onorato, Florence, 1957, p. 82, n. 94). The announcements always contained the name of the person giving the games (the *editor*), and they often gave the name of the gladiatorial *familia* as well. There was music as well: Trumpets, horns and tibias blew as the starting signal for the show. Great amphitheatres were also equipped with powerful water organs (*hydrauli*).

The first permanent amphitheatre in Rome was the Augustan amphitheatre of Statilius Taurus in the Campus Martius, but the terrible fire of 64 A.D. destroyed it. The Flavian emperors were the rulers responsible for endowing the city, at last, with the largest building dedicated to the spectacle in the entire ancient world. The Colosseum, originally called Amphitheatrum Flavium, had three arcaded stories, and a fourth story in masonry containing a series of large square windows flanked by pilasters. Its maximum axis measured 188 meters, its height was 50 meters, and its capacity, over 50,000 persons. To spread its immense segmented *velarium*, a team of 100 sailors from the nearby barracks (*Castra Misenantium*) had to be put to work on the monument's attic. The Amphitheatrum Flavium was erected in the valley where Nero had excavated an artificial lake for the Domus Aurea. A huge bed of concrete with a radius larger than the radius of the edifice was first poured into the basin of the lake. The foundations were built upon this concrete bed and consisted in the travertine pillars which formed the monument's load-bearing framework. The name Colosseum – probably deriving from the amphitheatre's proximity to the Colossus Neronis-Helios, which was situated in the vestibule of the Domus Aurea – was not an ancient name, and does not appear in documents before the year 1000.

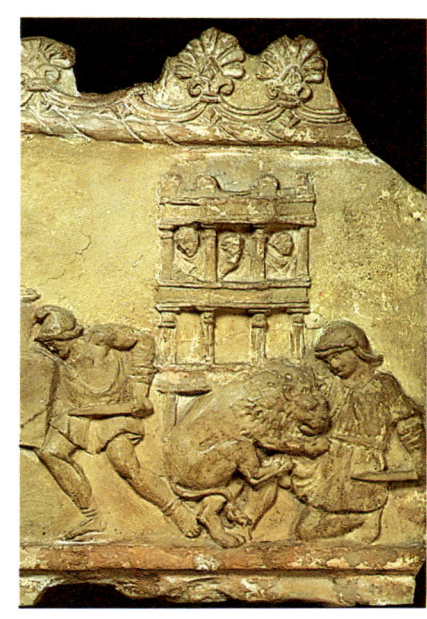

The external structure of the edifice, like the framework, was of travertine, laid dry; the interior was of dry tufa stonework; and the parts having a secondary static function were of brickwork. The arena pavement, which must have been of wood, rested upon the structures visible today: a network of corridors and rooms reserved for services and apparatuses relating to stage effects, whose degree of sophistication was great enough to permit wild beasts and other elements of the scene – stage sets such as hills, trees, lakes and the like – to pass through trapdoors and appear simultaneously in the arena. They were used especially for the *venationes*, the wild animal "hunts" generally paired with regular gladiatorial fights during the Empire.

The *cavea*, or sitting area, consisted of three tiers of masonry steps and a last tier in wood. Each section was reserved by law for a certain class of the population; inscriptions indicating section assignments can still be found on surviving tiers. Since the spectacles were free and open to everyone, people began lining up

95. *The riot of 59 B.C. between the Pompeiians and their Nucerian neighbors. Naples, National Archaeological Museum.*

96. *Detail of a relief with circus scenes. Milan, Scala Theatrical Museum.*

97. *Terracotta statuettes representing gladiators. Taranto, National Archaeological Museum.*

## City Streets and Shops

Roman city streets and out-of-town highways were composed of a multi-strata foundation covered by a finishing surface layer. The *statumen* was the foundation base, made up of large, loose rocks. Above it, a mixture of smaller stones and mortar was poured on to create a 60-70 cm. thick layer, the *rudus*. A third, approximately 10 cm. thick layer, the *nucleus*, was spread over the *rudus*. It was also composed of a cement mixture, but with shards added to the mortar. Finally, nicely smoothed and finished large paving blocks of flintstone or limestone were set in place, fitting together perfectly and forming the *pavimentum*, the surface pavement.

Sewage conduits ran along below the road at the level of the *statumen* and the *rudus* layers; lead pipes carrying water from the aqueduct to the large city reservoirs generally lay at less than a meter below the *pavimentum* surface (see: *Supplies*, p. 42).

The consular roads and out-of-town highways were about 4-4½ meters wide, reaching a width of 6 meters only on bridges or along curves; but the city streets were nearly all quite narrow and, since life during most of the day went on outside the home, they were crowded: "... hurry as I may, I am blocked by a surging crowd in front, and by a dense mass of people pressing in on us from behind; one man digs an elbow into me, another a hard sedan-pole; one bangs a beam, another a wine-cask against my head. My legs are beplastered with mud; soon huge feet trample on me from every side, and a soldier plants his hobnails firmly on my toe" (Juvenal, *Sat.* III, 243 ff.). Traffic was also heavy: Sedans and litters (the carriages of the rich), carts for the transportation of merchandise and heavy materials, and even flocks of sheep and herds of cattle clattered by.

At night, the streets were dark and unsafe, for there was no illumination, and those who went out had to carry a light of their own. Juvenal expounds: "And now regard the different and diverse perils of the night. See what a height it is to that towering roof from which a potsherd comes crack upon my head every time that some broken or leaky vessel is pitched out of the window! See with what a smash it strikes and dints the pavement! There's death in every open

I. *The Clivus Argentarius, behind the Forum Caesaris.*

II. *Via Biberatica, in Trajan's Market.*

III. *The 'tabernae' (shops) of Via Biberatica.*

IV. *Poultryman's shop sign. There are also rabbits in the hutches, and two monkeys on the counter. Ostia, Museum.*

V. *Greengrocer's shop sign. Ostia, Museum.*

window as you pass along at night...
[and]... you can but hope... that
they may be content to pour down on
you [only] the contents of their slop-
basins! [And here comes] your drun-
ken bully looking for a fight" (*Sat.* III,
268 ff.). Pliny the Younger lays it on
even thicker with his cases of people
who left their homes after dark and disappeared mysteriously into the night
(*Ep.* VI, 25 f.).

When the streets were lined with
shops, they became even less practica-
ble; for stands full of merchandise
protruded beyond the shop line, and
pedlars' stalls were set up especially
between the columns of the porticoed
streets. According to Martial, Domitian attempted to free the streets of
the intrusive shopkeepers' presence:
"Barber, taverner, cook, butcher keep
to their own thresholds. Now Rome
exists, of late it was a huge shop" (VII,
lxi, 9f.).

The shops (*tabernae*) ordinarily
consisted of a ground-storey room in
one of the large residential buildings
lining the streets. It had a masonry or
wooden counter for selling goods near
the entrance, and a back-room which
served for storage or living quarters.
Above the shop, there was almost always a mezzanine reached by a wood-
en ladder, whose first steps were occasionally built in masonry; and that
was the storekeeper's only home —
unless he struck it so rich that he
could afford another one.

All sorts of goods were sold in the
shops, from food-stuffs, to clothing, to
fabrics, to pots and pans, art objects,
jewellery and books (*scrinia librorum*,
Catullus, XIV, 17f.). Many shop premises were also used for other types of
businesses: There were laundries (*fullo-
nicae*) and dyehouses specialized in
purple, as well as tanneries, bakeries
and artisans' workshops with black-
smiths, bronze-workers, plumbers, pot-
ters, glassmakers, carpenters, inlayers,
engravers, silversmiths and gold-
smiths. Even the latter were not neces-
sarily wealthy, for the client often furnished the material for the job. There
were also 'banks' (*tabernae argentariae*)
where the prevalent activity was cur-
rency exchange; and, of course, taverns and eating-houses, bursting with
clients at all hours of the day and night
and the meeting place for gamblers
and bands of lusty young men (Catullus, XXXVII, 1 ff.) where one could
eat and drink one's fill.

*VI. Relief with city traffic. Stockholm, Na-
tional Museum. An important — probably
imperial — couple with an escort on horse-
back drives quickly through the city streets
in a chariot. A woman on a terrace is hanging or beating a rug or cloth.*

*VII. Banker's sign. Belgrade, National
Museum.*

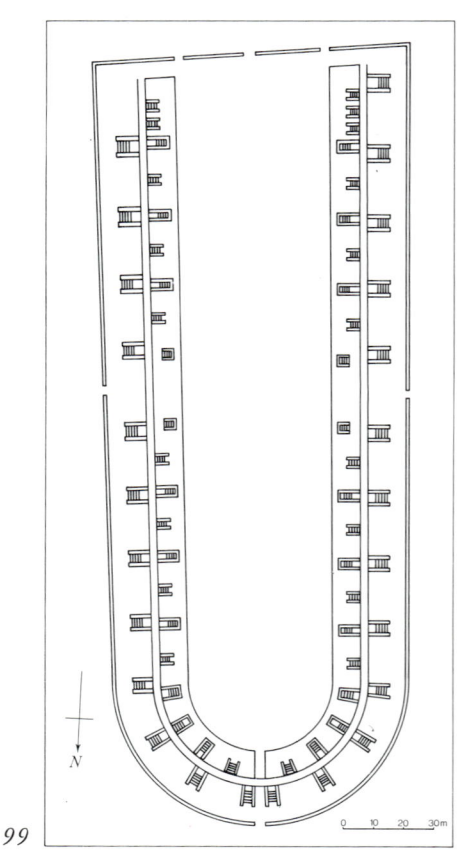

98. Relief showing a chariot race in the Circus Maximus. Foligno, Archaeological Museum.

99. Plan of Domitian's Stadium.

100. Aerial view of Piazza Navona showing the area where the ancient Stadium of Domitian once stood.

for a good seat the night before the show. Women attended the combats too, although for the duration of the Augustan morality-improvement campaign they were relegated to the last, wooden row to avoid promiscuity. But under the principate, in the age of prosperity and conspicuous consumption, some women were prepared to face ruin in order to appear in the amphitheatre looking like a great lady: "Ogulnia hires clothes to see the games; she hires attendants, a litter, cushions, female friends, a nurse, and a fair-haired girl to run her messages..." (Juvenal, *Sat.* VI, 352 f.).

Whether gladiatorial fights or wild animal hunts, these spectacles were inevitably savage and cruel, and they always ended up in a bloodbath. In 55 B.C., Cicero made note of an elephant massacre (*Ad fam.* VII, i, 3); in 80 A.D., in his *De spectaculis*, written for the inauguration of the Colosseum, Martial recorded the death of hundreds of gladiators and thousands of wild beasts in the one hundred days of games given by the emperor Titus. During periods of especially great moral laxity, even some women of good social standing made a spectacle of themselves in the arena and added an erotic touch to the fights: "Maevia, with spear in hand and breasts exposed [takes] to pig-sticking in Etruria..." (Juvenal, *Sat.* I, 22 f.; cf. II, 53 for women athletes and wrestlers).

Cheering for gladiators and general overexcitement during the fights reached the same frenzied pitch as they did at the circus games. A brawl might break out over nothing, as did the famous bloody riot between the townsfolk of Pompeii and their Nucerian neighbors (Tacitus, *Ann.* XIV, xvii); and a woman was capable of ruining her reputation over an athlete's muscles: "she will give all that remains of the family plate, down to the last flagon, to some smooth-faced athlete" – that is Juvenal's Ogulnia again (*Sat.* VI, 355 f.). Passion for the games was not restricted to the lower classes; it was widespread even among the educated. "Is the Thracian Chicken a match for Syrus?" chats Maecenas with Horace in his carriage (*Sat.* II, vi, 44); and in the 4th century A.D., Libanius, who always exhibited great boredom at the shows, nevertheless could often be

*101. Bas-relief with scene from a comedy. The actors are wearing masks. Naples, National Archaeological Museum.*

*102. Detail of a fresco from a house in Pompeii showing an actor from the comic theatre.*

*103. Detail of a mosaic depicting a mime dancing and playing the cymbals.*

104

105

104. *Theatre of Marcellus. To the right, the columns of the Augustan Temple of Apollo Sosianus.*

105. *Reconstruction of the Theatre of Marcellus. Rome, Museum of Roman Civilisation.*

found hard at work writing letters to ensure the success of games offered by his friends and relatives. Not even the first Christian emperors were willing to risk a loss of popularity by abolishing these fierce and bloody spectacles. It is true that Constantine forbade gladiatorial games in the East — but he did not forbid them in the West. And Valentinian III barely managed to ban them after 438 A.D. But the *venationes* survived. The last show on record was offered by Maximus, consul designate under Theodoric, in 523 A.D.

In Rome, the ruins of only one amphitheatre other than the Colosseum survive. They belong to the Amphitheatre Castrensis now incorporated into the Aurelian walls near the Church of Santa Croce in Gerusalemme and dating, perhaps, from the reign of Elagabalus. Its entire structure was brickwork, and its maximum diameter 88 meters.

Another magnificent type of spectacle was the *naumachia*, consisting of naval battles with real ships and, naturally, real deaths, and held in artificial lakes excavated for the purpose (the oldest was Caesar's in the Campus Martius, built in 46 B.C.) or else in the Colosseum, or in a stadium, like Domitian's, which occupied today's Piazza Navona. When the huge public buildings were used, they were filled with water for the event. Ordinarily, stadiums housed athletic competitions, the entertainment least popular with Romans.

Rome also had several theatres. The first masonry edifice to be built for theatrical use was Pompey's theatre, dedicated in 55 B.C.:

"Before, the games had usually been exhibited with the help of improvised tiers of benches and a stage thrown up for the occasion; or, to go further into the past, the people stood to watch: seats in the theatre, it was feared, might tempt them to pass whole days in indolence" (Tacitus, *Annals*, XIV, xx, 2-3). Thus, Romans saw the comedies of Plautus and Terence and the tragedies of Ennius, Naevius, Pacuvius and Accius performed on a wooden stage with a single set and three doors in the background and, when necessary, a small shrine (*fanum*). Towards the middle of the 1st century, however, these improvised theatres had become buildings which were sumptuous beyond compare. Pliny writes that when Marcus Scaurus was *aedile* (58 B.C.) "he constructed the greatest of all the works ever made by man, a work that surpassed not merely those erected for a limited period but even those intended to last forever. This was his theatre, which had a stage arranged in three storeys with 360 columns... The lowest storey of the stage was marble, and the middle one of glass (an extravagance unparalleled even in later times), while the top storey was made of gilded planks... The bronze statues in the spaces between the columns numbered 3000, as I mentioned earlier: As for the auditorium [*cavea*], it accomodated 80,000" (N.H. XXXVI, xxiv, 114 f.). And in 53 B.C., Curio, for the funeral games in honor of his father, "built close to each other two very large wooden theatres, each poised and balanced on a revolving pivot. During the forenoon, a performance of a play was given in both of

106. *Mosaic with theatrical masks. Rome, Capitoline Museum.*

107. *The Theatre of Ostia Antica.*

# Personal Hygiene

In each and every period of Roman history, citizens regarded personal hygiene (*cura corporis*) as a matter of very great concern: A daily bath, usually taken in the afternoon, was a regular habit among nearly all social classes. In the Late Empire, Rome had as many as eleven magnificent free public baths or *thermae* and over 830 admission-free or very low-priced private baths, spread throughout the various neighborhoods of the city. In many of the large rental apartment buildings there were small *thermae* on the ground floor for the tenants; while the homes of the rich were equipped with their own often quite sumptuous private baths.

In the Republican era, according to Seneca: "there were few baths, and they were not fitted out with any display... The bathers of those days did not have water poured over them, nor did it always run fresh as if from a hot spring; and they did not believe that it mattered at all how perfectly pure was the water into which they were to leave their dirt... [Scipio] did not bathe in filtered water; it was often turbid, and after heavy rains almost muddy! But it did not matter much to Scipio if he had to bathe in that way; he went there to wash off sweat, not ointment... Friend, if you were wiser, you would know that Scipio did not bathe every day. It is stated by those who have reported to us the old-time ways of Rome that the Romans washed only their arms and legs daily (because those were the limbs which gathered dirt in their daily toil) and bathed all over only once a week" (*Ep. Mor.* LXXXVI, 9-12).

During the Empire, on the other hand, "Your great man will spend six hundred thousand sesterces upon his baths" (Juvenal, *Sat.* VII, 178; cf. Martial IX, 75); that was quite a fortune!

In the days of the Late Empire, the Church cast a disapproving eye upon the baths, and decidedly condemned the mixed baths, which were open to both men and women. "He who has been bathed once in Christ has no need of a second bath" wrote St. Jerome (*Ep.* 14 § 10); and St. Augustine authorized nuns to visit the baths but once a month (*Ep.* 211 § 13). "If a man is in good health, a bath will spoil and weaken his body and lead to lust" decreed the hermit, Barsanufius (*Bibl.*, ed Volo, 1960, p. 336). But love for the baths was so great among the Romans that Church censure was long ignored, almost universally — even by the clergy. Look at the answer given at the end of the 4th century by Sisinnius, bishop of Constantinople, to the question why he, a priest, bathed twice a day: "Because I haven't time for three", he said (Socrates, *Hist. Eccl.* VI, 22).

Apart from the widespread practice of depilation and the use of oils and greases and perfumes on the body, there were only a few other rituals of personal hygiene. One cleaned one's ears with vinegar (Persius, *Sat.* V, 86) and one took care of one's teeth. Catullus refers with disgust to one Egnatius, who washed his teeth each morning with urine, according to the Spanish fashion, to make them a bright and shiny white. (XXXVII, 20 and XXXIX, 20 f.).

Since the inadequacy of razors made it impossible for men to shave themselves well, they went to the barber (*tonsor*), whose perenially crowded shop was always abuzz with the latest news and gossip of the city. Hair-removal was executed with a sort of poultice called *dropax* (Martial X, 65, 8), or with resinous depilatory 'waxes' (Martial XII, 32, 21 f.); or even with curved tweezers (*forcipes aduncae*). And in the 1st century A.D., the vainest men practiced whole-body depilation: "what manner is this of removing the hair from one's pubes and from the secret regions of one's loins to display openly one's faded pudenda" (Persius, *Sat.* IV, 35 f.).

In addition to public baths, there were also public toilets (*foricae*) in the *thermae*, in great architectural complexes, and in the large apartment buildings. One is still visible in Caesar's Forum, above the ground floor shops fronting on the square. It is a large semicircular room containing heating equipment and a long marble counter with holes running along the semicircular wall.

All these public facilities helped to relieve the discomfort caused by the lack of running water in individual living units. Romans got water from public fountains on the streets or from private fountains in the courtyards of the apartment buildings that were equipped with them. And since drainage and sewage pipes were not installed everywhere, basinsfuls of liquid occasionally rained down from the windows (Juvenal, *Sat.* III, 277).

Garbage collection services were supervised by the *curatores viarum* — the road magistrates (see: *Monument Maintenance*, p. 20).

*I. A great arcade from the Baths of Caracalla.*

*II. Aerial view of the Baths of Caracalla.*

*III. Water heater. Naples, National Archaeological Museum.*

*IV. 'Forica' (privy) from Ostia.*

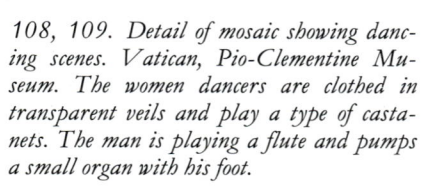

108, 109. *Detail of mosaic showing dancing scenes. Vatican, Pio-Clementine Museum. The women dancers are clothed in transparent veils and play a type of castanets. The man is playing a flute and pumps a small organ with his foot.*

them and they faced in opposite directions so that the two casts should not drown out each other's words. Then all of a sudden the theatres revolved (and it is agreed that after the first few days they did so with some of the spectators actually remaining in their seats), their corners met, and thus Curio provided an amphitheatre in which he produced fights between gladiators..." (Pliny, *N.H.* XXXVI, xxiv, 117).

The theatres in masonry erected at the end of the 1st century B.C. included the Theatre of Marcellus, which with its three arcaded tiers was a sort of precursor of the Colosseum, standing near the Temple of Apollo Sosianus; and the Theatre of Balbus in the ninth region. Later, Trajan built another theatre, in the Campus Martius; but his successor, Hadrian, had it demolished.

The Roman and Greek theatres differed in a number of ways. For example, in the theatres of Rome the semicircular cavea with its tiered seats rested upon masonry structures instead of a natural slope; and the stage could be transformed into a very high, multi-storied wall, decorated with columns, niches and statues, and containing the *pulpitum*, a platform towards the front on which the actors performed. The *aulaeum*, a cloth curtain richly adorned with figures, was used to close off the stage. Virgil mentions one which was decorated with the tale of Caesar's expedition in Britannia (*Georgics*, III, 25). These illustrated curtains did not open toward the sides of the stage or rise as theatre curtains do today. Rather, they were gathered into a deep groove at the foot of the stage wall: "So when on festal days the curtain in the theatre is raised, figures of

Public Buildings

*110. Mosaic of theatrical scene showing the actors and mimes. Naples, National Archaeological Museum.*

men [which decorate it] rise up, showing first their faces, then little by little all the rest; until at last, drawn up with steady motion, the entire forms stand revealed, and plant their feet upon the curtain's edge" (Ovid, *Metam.*, III, 111 ff.).

As for theatre repertory (*ludi scaenici*), the classical Greek tragedies and comedies as well as the works of the great early Republican poets (Ennius, Naevius, Pacuvius, Plautus, Terence, etc.) were eliminated quite early. By the 1st century B.C., cultural and political degradation had so thoroughly transformed the urban population that it was beyond recognition. The most successful theatrical genres were mime and pantomime. Mime shows presented undemanding tales of adventure spiced up with an abundance of licentiousness and, all too soon, elements of horror taken from the gladiatorial fights so popular with the crowds. Actors beat and wounded each other quite realistically on the stage and, when necessary, live prisoners under sentence of death were brought in to show them dying amidst torture and great suffering. Pantomime, a show of masked dancers miming the action of a story whose subject was often mythological, was so typically Roman that the Greeks called it the 'Italian dance' – although it was introduced by two Greeks, Pylades of Cilicia and Bathyllus of Alexandria. Its cultural level was slightly above that of the mime, and it was much appreciated by the educated classes.

Actors, like athletes, aroused popular enthusiasm and caused incredible reactions. At the more risqué mime shows, where there were woman players, the populace shouted for its favorite actresses

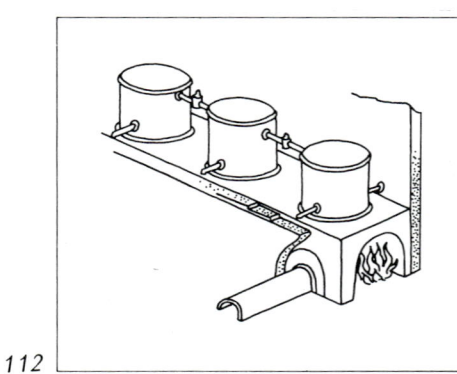

111. Trajan's Baths, a large exedra in the outer precinct.

112. Reconstruction of the heating system for water at the baths (from H. Plommer), according to Vitruvius' description (De Arch. V, 10, 1).

to show themselves naked upon the stage; and at the 'Italian dance', where male actors took women's parts: "When the soft Bathyllus dances the part of gesticulating Leda, Tuccia cannot contain herself; your Apulian maiden heaves a sudden and longing yelp of ecstasy, as though she were in a man's arms; the rustic Thymele is all attention; it is then that she 'learns her lesson'" (Juvenal, *Sat.* VI, 63 ff.). Nothing could be further from the scurrility of Plautus or the innocent insults of Sarmentus and Messius Cicirrus in Horace's famous story of a battle of country wits (*atellana*) (*Sat.* I, V, 51-70). Yet, even St. Augustine in the 4th century had to confess to his passion for the mime: "Theatrical performances held me in thrall with their images of my misery and their bait for the fire that burned within me. What may this be? Man desires suffering when he attends the theatre and witnesses the unravelling of tragic and painful events which, however, he would never wish to endure. Still, the spectator wants a taste of the pain; in fact, that very pain represents his enjoyment" (*Confessions* III, 2).

But, in addition to the entertainment which amphitheatre, circus and theatre provided (and they all had very high attendances; for the peak number of holidays in Imperial Rome was 182 a year, and no holiday was without its own special games) the city of Rome offered its inhabitants an important daily distraction: The public baths (see: *Personal Hygiene*, p. 54).

Baths (*balnea*), both public baths and private baths in the homes of the rich, had existed in Rome ever since the Republic. But originally they were dark, uncomfortable places designed in accordance with functional rather than aesthetic criteria. On the whole,

Public Buildings

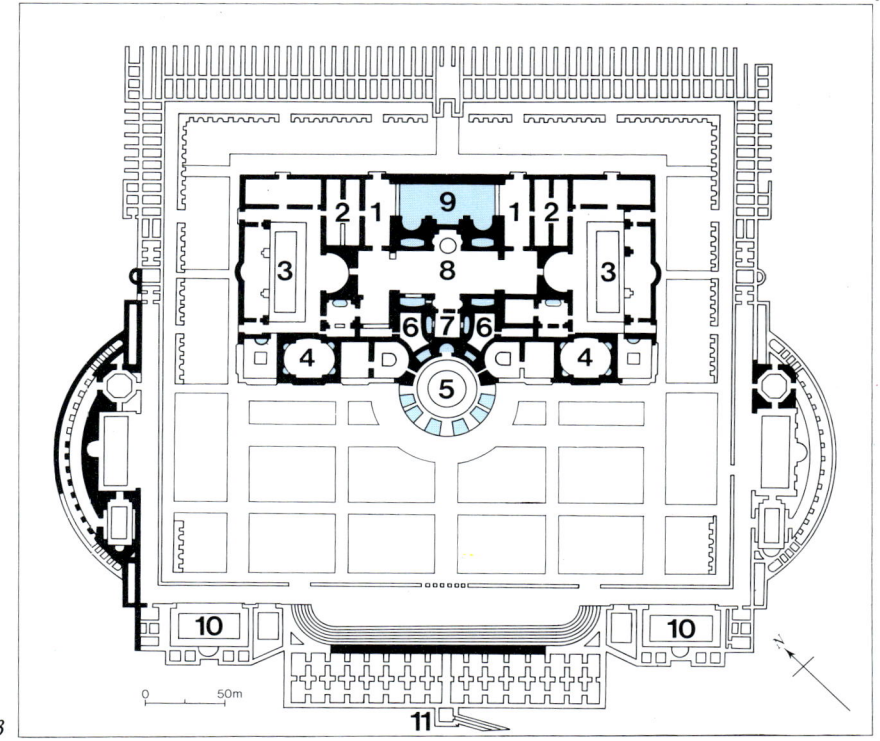

their floor plans imitated older Greek models. But when Agrippa built the first *thermae* in the Campus Martius in 25 B.C. (followed by Nero's *thermae*, between 62 and 64 A.D.) the old-style baths immediately went out of fashion. Seneca comments on the situation at that time in a letter to Lucilius, written from an old bathing establishment: "In this bath of Scipio's there are tiny chinks (you cannot call them windows) cut out of the stone wall in such a way as to admit light without weakening the fortifications; nowadays, however, people regard baths as fit for moths if they have not been so arranged that they receive the sun all day long through the widest of windows, if men cannot bathe and get a coat of tan at the same time, and if they cannot look out from their bath-tubs over stretches of land and sea. So it goes; the establishments which had drawn crowds and had won admiration when they were first opened are avoided and put back in the category of venerable antiques as soon as luxury has worked out some new device, to her own ultimate undoing" (*Ep. Mor.*, LXXXVI, 8).

The monumental baths were a completely Roman invention. In a city which in no time at all had become the capital of a vast empire and whose constantly increasing population was crowded into intensive housing units lacking sanitary facilities, the invention in all likelihood originated in a real, pressing need. Architecturally, the *thermae* were designed in accordance with principles of strict symmetry. Four elements were lined up along the central axis: 1) the *natatio* or open pool, 2) the hall with tubs for the *frigidarium* or cold bath, 3) a smaller hall with tubs for the *tepidarium* or warm bath, 4) the hall with tubs for the *caldarium* or hot bath. To the right and left of this central line was a number of other rooms serving for complementary activities: changing rooms (*apodyteria*); massage and depilation rooms; and sauna and turkish bath facilities (*laconica*),

113. Plan of the Baths of Caracalla
 1. Entrance
 2. Changing rooms
 3. Gymnasia
 4. Special baths
 5. Caldarium
 6. Courtyards
 7. Tepidarium
 8. Frigidarium or Basilica
 9. Open-air swimming pool (natatio)
 10. Libraries
 11. Water tanks

114. Detail of mosaic from the Baths of Caracalla showing one of the judges of the games held there. Vatican, Gregorian Profane Museum.

# Education

Schooling in Rome increased considerably in the period between Augustus' and Marcus Aurelius' reigns. Vespasian was the first emperor to create the role of the teacher as public servant, paid by the state. Between 133 and 136, Hadrian unified the city schools of higher education in a single edifice called the *Athenaeum* – the Academy. Throughout the Empire period, Rome was the only great cultural center of the Latin West.

Instruction was divided into three levels: Primary school, grammar school and rhetoric school.

Primary schools were private institutions. The teacher (the *litterarius* or *ludi magister*) was of modest social standing. He taught reading and, with the help of the abacus, arithmetic, to boys and girls of 7 to 14 years of age.

Generally, lessons were held outdoors, either beneath the portico or loggia (*pergula*) of the rented apartment buildings, or in a public area. For example, wall graffiti tell us that lessons were held in the Basilica Argentaria of Caesar's Forum; and the exedra of Trajan's great forum served as a schoolroom too.

Naturally, these were schools for lower class and poor children; the sons and daughters of the rich received their primary education at home. The teacher was paid by his pupils' parents, and the sum he received was a very modest one. In Diocletian's *Edictum de pretiis* (VII, 66, the Edict of prices), the teacher's wage was set at 50 *denarii* a month per pupil. If one only considers that the salary of an artisan was 50-60 *denarii* a day, one will clearly see how large elementary school classes had to be in order for the teacher to reach the standard of living of a mason or a carpenter. On the other hand, much was expected of him: Not only was he required to possess a healthy dose of erudition; but he had to "mould the young minds as a man moulds a face out of wax with his thumb" and to "be a father to the whole brood". But, when the end of the year came round, he was to receive only "the golden piece which the mob demands for a winning jockey" (Juvenal, *Sat.* VII, 230 ff.). Teaching methods were based on rote learning and memorization. Saint Augustine recalls how bored he was at school when he was required to repeat with the monotony of a nursery rhyme, "unum et unum, duo; duo et duo, quattuor..." (*Conf.* I, 20 and 22). The means of keeping the pupils' attention was the rod.

Few students reached the second level, where the teacher (the *grammaticus*) taught correct diction and the rules of grammar from Greek and Latin classical texts, which the pupils were made to memorize. Contemporary poets were also read in the schools (Persius, *Sat.* I, 29).

The *rethor*, in the third level, taught the art of rhetoric. Students not only had to study rules and analyze texts; they also had to write and recite compositions. Persius writes: "I used often, I remember, as a boy, to smear my eyes with oil in order to appear ill and avoid going to school, and thus I would be saved from reciting the noble speech of the dying Cato – a speech which would be much applauded by my idiot of a master, and that to which my father, sweating with delight, would have to listen with his invited friends" (Persius, *Sat.* III, 44 ff.). The subjects of exercises were drawn exclusively from mythology or ancient history – and never from contemporary life. Here is a typical theme: "after Chaeronea, Philip promises to release two thousand prisoners in exchange for Demosthenes; Demosthenes asks to be surrendered to Philip". The result was an essentially literary and linguistic culture, with vague notions of history, geography, philosophy and antiquity.

Side by side with the 'state' teachers were private teachers, for anyone could open a school of grammar or rhetoric. The cost, in the Diocletian price edict, was 200-250 *denari* a pupil. But the venture was not a very safe one, for at the end of the academic year many students vanished into thin air without paying a single *denarius*. This immoral behavior was especially widespread in Rome (St. Augustine, *Conf.*, V, 22). Diplomas and exams were nonexistent; and the duration of courses depended on the pupils' interest.

Beyond the third level of education, there were specialized 'universities' in certain cities. In Rome, one could study philosophy and jurisprudence. Jurisprudence was the first course to adopt a formal diploma, a diploma which was indispensible for the practice of law at the end of the 5th century.

One of the most popular specializations was medicine, which one could study in Athens or in Alexandria. In the Late Empire, physicians were given equal status with state teachers. In Rome, the most important doctors were the court doctors, the *archiatri sacri palatii*; then came the public physicians, whose role was established by Valentinian I. These medical men could not ask fees of their patients, but had to "minister to the poor honorably rather than ... serve the rich shamefully" (*CTh*, XIII, 3, 8, year 368). Of course, there were also private medical practices.

When the Church became State-controlled, a strong current of Christian thought was opposed to the use of the classics as the basis for Roman instruction. St. Jerome dreamed of finding himself before the seat of God in judgment, and there he was condemned for his pagan culture: "I was asked to state my condition and replied that I was a Christian. But He who presided said: 'Thou liest; thou art a Ciceronian, not a Christian. For where thy treasure is there will thy heart be also'" (*Ep.* 22, § 30).

But tradition was so strong that all through the 6th century programs remained as they were; and Christian boys and girls continued to memorize pagan genealogies and the amorous adventures of Jove.

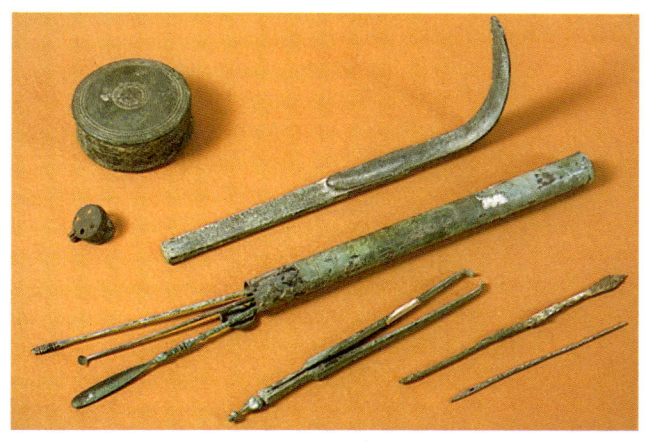

*I. Small Roman abacus. Rome, Museo delle Terme*

*II. Relief showing a secretarial school ('notarii'). Ostia, Museum.*

*III. Relief showing a childbirth scene. Ostia, Museum.*

*IV. Surgical instruments from the Tomb of the Surgeon. Este, Museo Nazionale Atestino.*

*V. Fresco depicting an anatomy lesson. Rome, Catacomb of Via Latina.*

*VI. Sarcophagus of the 'gens Sosia' showing a patient being treated by an oculist. Ravenna, National Museum. Eye ailments were quite common in antiquity. In Rome, in the morning, the crowding of oculist's offices was second only to that of the barber's shops.*

*115. The 'Frigidarium' of the Baths of Neptune at Ostia.*

*116. The circular hall of the Baths of the Seven Sages at Ostia.*

alternatively used for special baths, such as the medicinal baths used in treating skin diseases. The *thermae* were also equipped with gymnasiums (huge courtyards enclosed by porticoes) and with exedrae with libraries and reading rooms, and with club rooms, lecture halls, and even 'restaurants' where bath-goers could eat. Architects also took into account building exposure; for the outer walls of the *caldarium*, which had large windows, generally faced southwest.

The heart of the *thermae*, in which the alternation of rooved, walled buildings and narrow shafts or courtyards permitted all of the rooms to receive daylight and sunlight, generally lay at the center of a garden surrounded in turn by a porticoed structure containing along its perimeter exedrae and other edifices, as well as the great reservoirs used to collect the water.

The bath halls (especially the magnificently large main halls, such as the *caldarium* of Caracalla's baths, with its 34 meter diameter) contained in their interior a wealth of decorative elements: polychrome marbles, columns, statues, stuccoes, floor mosaics. A network of corridors in the basement below permitted attendants to move quickly from one end of the building to the other and to expedite all necessary services with ease. Water for the hot baths was heated to the required temperature by a wood furnace and boiler system connected to the *caldarium* by tubes. The hot air produced by combustion was simultaneously carried to the rooms that needed heating, by a tunnel which ran beneath the upstairs flooring.

The great *thermae* of Rome were built by Titus, Trajan, Caracalla and Diocletian. Nothing but a plan drawn by Palladio survives of Titus' Baths; of Trajan's, a few glorious ruins remain on the slopes of the Oppian Hill. But Caracalla's and Diocletian's Baths were the most magnificent. The former, which measured 337 x 328 meters with its outer structures and porticoes and had a central nucleus of bath buildings measuring 220 x 114 meters was supplied with water from one of the branches of the great Aqua Marcia aqueduct, and could accomodate nearly 1,500 persons at a time. The latter, with its 380 x 370 meters large grounds and its 250 x 180 meters bath buildings, also received water from the Marcian Acqueduct, and could simultaneously serve 3,000 persons.

To get an idea of the magnificence of Diocletian's *thermae* one must enter the Basilica of Santa Maria degli Angeli. The great niches facing on Piazza della Repubblica belonged to the baths' *caldarium*; the present-day basilica entrance was the *tepidarium*; and the church itself was the *frigidarium* or *basilica*. The semicircular exedra described by the buildings now on the square nearly corresponds to the exedra of the ancient *thermae* enclosure (it is somewhat smaller). The entire complex spread over 13 hectares of land.

The last great baths of Rome were built by Constantine, on the Quirinal, and by his mother, Helen (Thermae Helenianae), on the eastern slopes of the Caelian Hill. Nothing remains of the former, and very little is left of the latter.

*117. Baths of Diocletian, aerial view.*

Just as the forum basilicas and the porticoes lining the streets and squares were the Roman's favorite morning haunts, the grandiose bathing establishments were his chosen afternoon resort. The huge *frigidarium* hall was the basilica of the *thermae*, and in it people of all stations and walks of life met and mingled; occasionally, even an emperor put in an appearance. In Rome, the men of power and the poorest of the poor were united by a passion for physical exercise and bathing; some foolhardy fellows were even rash enough to jump in right after a meal: "But you will soon pay for it, my friend, when you take off your clothes, and with distended stomach carry your peacock into the bath undigested ..." (Juvenal, *Sat.*, I, 142 ff.).

In his treatise on medicine (*De methodo medendi*, XI, 15), Galen recommends a sauna first, then a hot bath, and finally, after a warm bath, a cold water swim. And that was precisely the customary itinerary of the great *thermae*. One passed from the dressing-room near the entrance to the gymnasium porticoes where the physically fit could stop and take their exercise; then one walked on to the heated rooms alongside the *caldarium* and, after a hot bath, returned to the exit by following the building's central axis to the large outdoor pool; finally one proceeded to the changing room to retrieve the clothing left behind at the start.

But these enormous establishments offered numberless possibilities for distraction. No wonder that the citizens of Rome whiled away whole afternoons there.

118. *The nymphaeum of the Domus of Cupid and Psyche in Ostia.*

119. *A room in the Domus of Cupid and Psyche in Ostia.*

120. *Plan of the House of Pansa at Pompeii. It is a typical example of an atrium-and-peristyle house.*

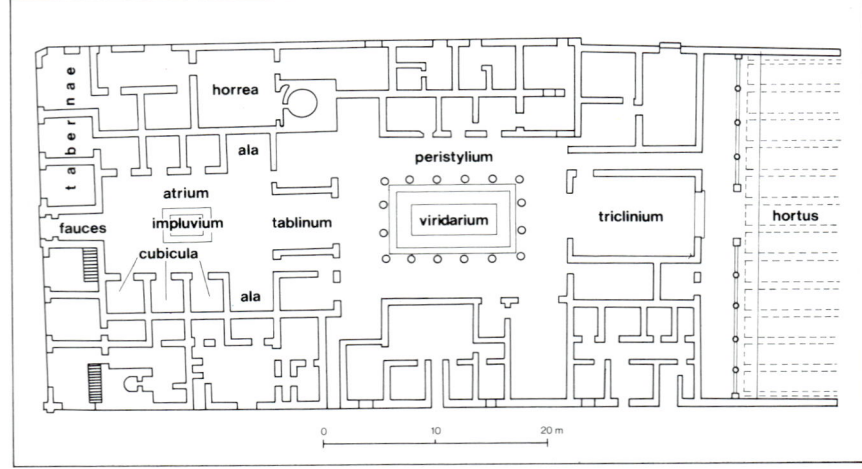

## Homes and Housing

The historical links that once stood between the iron-age *capanne* on the Palatine, the first homes of *Roma quadrata*, and the oldest surviving masonry houses are no longer in our possession. We know from literary sources (Varro, *De ling. lat.*, VI, 162) and from archaeological findings in other cities, such as Pompeii, that atrium-type housing spread early (from the 4th century B.C.) throughout the cities of Italy, and was certainly in use in Rome. It was planned around a central court or atrium, which had a series of rooms serving for family living facing upon it.

The basic schema included: An entrance door, the *ostium*, situated on the street side of the house, with or without a vestibule before it, and leading into a narrow corridor, the *fauces*, which ran from the door to the *atrium*. Beside the door there was generally a number of rooms facing onto the street and serving as shops (*tabernae*). The atrium had along its sides a series of small bedrooms (the *cubicula*) and, at the last, two open halls, the *alae*, which provided a passageway to the other chambers, including the service quarters, located behind the *cubicula*. On the far side of the atrium were the living rooms. The largest, central one was called the *tablinum*.

Ordinarily, the atrium court was partially covered by an overhanging roof built to carry water to the *impluvium*, a basin in the floor designed to catch rainwater and connected to an underground reservoir. It is clear, then, that all the rooms of the house faced inward, towards the atrium at the center, while on the outside there were high surrounding walls with practically no openings – except for the ground-floor shops, when they were present.

The atrium house was a rich man's house, a *domus*; but when the renewed prosperity of the 2nd century made aristocratic families even richer and lent to their life-style the elegance and refinement of Greece, the atrium *domus* was no longer sufficient. Enlargements were generally longitudinal, and consisted in the addition of a new building, planned around a portico called the *peristylium*, whose architectural origins were Hellenistic (Vitruvius, *De arch.* VI, 3 ff.). The peristyle dislodged the kitchen garden (*hortus*), which was reborn as a small arbor at the center of the portico, frequently enhan-

*121. Palatine, House of the Grifi. Room with wall paintings of the earliest phase of the 2nd style. Rome, Antiquarium of the Palatine.*

ced by fountains (*vividarium*). As in the atrium residence, the small rooms were located along the sides of the portico and the living rooms faced the entrance, with the *triclinium* or dining room at the center.

Republican sources of the last century before the fall describe many *domus* of this type. Some of the most famous were on the Palatine: That of Quintus Lutatius Catulus, conqueror of the Cimbri; that of Silla, richly decorated with oriental furnishings and Greek works of art; that of Emilius Scaurus, who adorned his residence with marble columns; that of the ill-famed Clodius; that of Cicero, who did so much to defend it during the dark days of the civil struggles (*De domo sua*); that of his brother Quintus; that of the orator Licinius; that of the triumvir Marcus Antonius, later the property of Agrippa; and that of the Octavians, where Augustus was born (Suetonius, *Div. Aug.* V). Atticus, Cicero's best friend, lived on the Quirinal, in a beautiful house, full of works of art, where refined banquets were regularly offered to a host of guests.

All these Republican residences were later replaced by those of the Imperial era. Very few remains have emerged from excavation work on the Palatine.

An example of the 2nd-century *domus* is the Casa dei Grifi, decorated with early 2nd-style paintings dating from the period spanning the 2nd and 1st centuries B.C., and the large room known as the 'Aula Isiaca', decorated with late 2nd-style paintings (*ca.* 25 B.C., see: *Mural Paintings*, p. 78).

There are also some late Republican rooms surviving on the Palatine, between the Temple of Magna Mater and the Temple of

122. *Bronze tripod and basin. Naples, National Archaeological Museum.*

123. *Oil lamp. Rome, Museum of Roman Civilisation.*

124. *Palatine, the so-called Aula Isiaca with late 2nd-style frescoes. Rome, Antiquarium of the Palatine.*

Apollo. Today it is believed (in all likelihood, correctly) that these were several houses later grouped together and readapted for use as Augustus' residence. Suetonius writes, "He lived at first near the Forum Romanum, above the stairs of the Ringmakers, in a house which had belonged to the orator Calvus; afterwards, on the Palatine, but in the no less modest dwelling of Hortensius, which was remarkable neither for size nor elegance, having but short colonnades with columns of Alban stone, and rooms without any marble decorations or handsome pavements. For more than forty years he used the same bedroom in winter and summer; although he found the city unfavourable to his health in the winter, yet he continued to winter there. If ever he planned to do anything in private or without interruption, he had a room in which to retire at the top of the house, which he called 'Syracuse' and 'little workshop' [*technyphion*]. In this he used to take refuge, or else in the villa of one of his freedmen in the suburbs; but whenever he was not well, he slept at Maecenas' house" (*Div. Aug.* LXXII, 1ff.).

Today, this residence of Augustus' appears to be divided into several living areas. They consist of an apartment to the northeast, traditionally called the House of Livia; a large peristyle at the center, with a suite of small family rooms towards the west; and following these, several state reception chambers which

*125. Palatine, House of Livia, 2nd-style wall.*

were open at the south and paved with marble alongside the portico of the temple of Apollo (House of Augustus). All of these structures once belonged to more ancient buildings; but they seem utterly transformed by readaptation. It is now difficult indeed to find traces of an atrium or peristyle *domus* plan in the two surviving apartments, although their rooms are assigned the conventional names *tablinum, triclinium*, etc. The mural decoration, on the other hand, contains highly interesting exemplars of the late 2nd style, with false architecture breaking through the wall plane, huge paintings depicting mythological subjects (*megalographiae*), and reproductions of actual theatrical stage-sets (Room of the Masks). The division of decorative syntax in the paintings into three parts corresponds perfectly with Vitruvius' description (see: *Mural Paintings*, p. 78).

Generally speaking, what surprises modern-day visitors to surviving homes are the relatively small size of nearly all the rooms, the fact that most of them are absolutely devoid of windows and therefore of light, and the inclusion among them of many decidedly mean, cramped cubicles. The need for store-rooms and pantries to compensate for the lack of furniture (especially of wardrobes and cupboards, see: *Home Furnishings*, p. 68) accounts for the presence of the last category of rooms. The small size of the living quarters and the dearth of natural lighting, on the other hand, may be taken as the tokens of two separate and distinct factors in Roman life.

The first was a practical problem: It consisted in the difficulty of

# Home Furnishings

The furnishings of Roman homes were for the most part built into the actual structure: There were wall niches, shelves or small cupboards made to hold various objects and food supplies, and sometimes even beds and tables built in masonry.

In fact, wood, bronze and marble furniture was absolutely secondary; and since rooms were generally small, even in elegant homes it was kept down to a bare minimum. In the dining room (*triclinium*), there were *lecti* (or beds) usually arranged in a horseshoe. These beds were the most important and handsome pieces of furniture in the house. They were made either of wood with bronze sculptural ornamentation or entirely of bronze, and had turned legs and head-rests or *fulcra*. During the Empire, the head-rests were as high as couch-backs and gave the beds the appearance of divans. The most beautiful *lecti* were manufactured in Southern Italy.

Each bed could seat up to three people; and a small round table of wood, bronze, stone or even silver with three animal's-paw legs was placed beside every group of dinner guests.

In the course of the Empire, the *triclinium* beds were frequently supplanted by *sigma*, a single bed accomodating all the guests, named after the C-shaped Greek character for S. It was semicircular in shape, built of either wood or masonry, and hidden beneath spreads and cushions.

Chairs or *sellae* were common, including folding chairs and *cathedrae* – armchairs with outcurving legs and feline-paw-shaped feet. In the Late Empire (5th-6th century A.D.), a basket-shaped wicker armchair with a high back, known in barbarian circles as early as the 3rd century, became extremely popular.

Settle trunks, coffers with pitched two-slope covers, wooden wardrobes and low credenzas with a shelf above and two cabinet doors below were the most commonly used storage compartments.

Chandeliers composed of several oil lamps; candlesticks with a decorated shaft and three animal-shaped feet as a base (often genuine works of art) and tripods, to hold large vases or lamps, generally in bronze and resting on three legs: All were objects belonging to Roman home furnishing.

Tapestries and draperies played an important role in interior decoration, but the enrichment of the rooms was due, above all, to wall paintings which, with their play of illusionistic perspective, enlarged the straitened spaces of the interiors (see: *Mural Paintings*, p. 78). Accompanying the paintings were floor mosaics and, in the more sumptuous *domus*, marble inlays on both walls and floors.

The homes of the rich were also embellished with works of art, and the passion for collecting existed already. Statius, speaking of Vindex's collection, mentioned "a thousand beauties of bronze and ancient ivory" (*Silv.* IV, 6); Pliny the Younger displayed great pride in his purchase of a Corinthian bronze realistically representing an old man (*Ep.* III, 6); and Silius Italicus spent a fortune on statues and busts and on books as well (Pliny the Younger, *Ep.* III, 7).

But the homes of the poor residing in the huge rental apartment buildings (the *insulae*) were not quite so lucky. Here is Martial's description of the possessions of a tenant evicted for arrears in his rent: "There went along a three-legged truckle-bed and a two-legged table, and, alongside a lantern and a bowl of cornel, a cracked chamberpot was leaking water through its broken side; the neck of a flagon was lying under a brazier green with verdigris; that there were salted gudgeons, too, or worthless sprats, the obscene stench of a jug confessed – such a stench as a whiff of a marine fish-pond would scarcely equal. Nor was there wanting a section of Tolosan cheese, nor a four-year-old chaplet of black pennyroyal, and ropes shorn of their garlic and onions, nor your mother's pot full of foul resin, the depilatory used by the women of the neighborhood. Why do you look for a house and tease rent-collectors when you can lodge for nothing, o Vacerra? This procession of your traps befits Beggar's bridge" (XII, xxxii, 11 ff.; cf. Juvenal, *Sat.* III, 10: "... his goods and chattels were packed upon a single wagon ...").

*III*

*IV*

*V*

*VI*

I. *Silver tableware. Naples, National Archaeological Museum.*

II. *Capitoline bisellium. Rome, Palace of the Conservators.*

III. *Floor mosaic with a basket of flowers. Vatican, Pio-Clementine Museum.*

IV. *Basket-shaped armchair in a relief from Neumagen. Treviri, Museum.*

V, VI. *Sarcophagus from Simpelveld. Leiden, Museum. Inside the sarcophagus is a relief showing a furnished bedroom: Beside the bed, an armchair on one side; and coffers with a two-slope cover, for clothing and linen, on the other. Against the other wall, shelves for vessels, a console table with three feline feet, cupboards and a bookcase.*

126. Palatine, House of Augustus, the Room of the Masks with late 2nd-style paintings.

127. Palatine, House of Augustus, pantry.

heating a house in winter and of creating efficient fixtures. In effect, even the rich limited their heating to a hot air flow beneath the flooring of the baths and the reception rooms; and for window closures, they generally used large doors of wood or stone (*valvae*, see Vitruvius, *De arch*. VI, 3, 9) and only rarely diaphanous (but not perfectly transparent) panes of mica, alabaster and glass. Here is how Martial was treated when a guest at the home of a man of wealth: "That your orchard trees from Cilicia may not grow wan and dread the winter, nor too keen an air nip the tender boughs, glass casements facing the wintry south winds admit the clear suns and daylights undefiled. But to me is assigned a garret, shut in by an ill-fitting window, in which even Boreas himself would not care to abide. Is it in such a lodging you cruelly bid your old friend dwell? Then as the guest of one of your trees I shall be more protected" (VIII, xiv).

The second was related to social life and life style, and derived from a typical way of breaking up the day. The ancient Roman did not spend much time at home. In the morning he took care of political, economic or private affairs in the Forum; and in the afternoons he bathed at the *thermae* or went to a show. He went home only to dine, and above all to sleep at night.

Obviously, women spent more time in the house; but one must keep in mind that the Roman matron was a woman with enormous liberty. Even before the days of the Twelve Tables, all laws which placed a wife under her husband's authority had been abolished; and marriages could be dissolved without legal formalities or state participation (except where *confarreatio* was involved) simply at the free will and pleasure of either party. From earliest times, the mistress of a household was not only in charge of domestic affairs; she also had control of family business when her husband was absent. She was generally educated and, if her social position was high, she often exerted a great deal of influence in public affairs. Cicero, in difficult times, wrote to the son of Claudius Marcellus and Junia, "I am fully conscious of the energetic support (more than should have been demanded of any woman) given to my welfare and position by that most sterling and excellent lady, your mother" (*Ad fam.* XV, vii).

Women also had comparative freedom in their relations with the other sex. They sat at table with husband and guests, they walked the city streets on their own, they went to the *thermae* and public entertainments alone; and, at times, they even defied social conventions, as did the Clodia, stigmatized by Cicero as the 'Palatine Medea', taken up in a constant whirlwind of parties, concerts and receptions in her riverbank 'villa', surrounded by a throng of admirers, and immortalized by her lover Catullus in his Lesbia poems.

Women's freedom increased during the Empire. Its excesses are evident in the escapades of certain famous empresses (Messalina, Faustina) and imperial concubines (Acte, Caenis, etc.). Procreation, on the other hand, decreased. Augustan marriage-protection and demographical-growth legislation sounded a clear, early note of alarm. Abortion became a widespread practice, and only women of the poorer classes "endure the perils of childbirth, and all the troubles of nursing to which their lot condemns them; but how often does a gilded bed contain a woman that is lying in? So great is the skill, so powerful the drugs, of the abortionist, paid to murder mankind within the womb" (Juvenal, *Sat.* VI, 593 ff.).

But side by side with the vulgar, unscrupulous creatures of Petronius' *Satyricon* and Juvenal's sixth satire who, in the age of the principate, modelled an entire collection of female iniquities, there

128. *Roman house beneath the Basilica of San Giovanni and San Paolo, the so-called Hall of the Orant with 3rd-century A.D. frescoes.*

129. *Hot air distribution tubes behind the wall of a house in Ostia Antica.*

*130, 131. Two views of the Insula of the Charioteers in Ostia.*

*132. Ostia, Via dei Balconi, the ground floor of an insula, a typical multi-storied Roman apartment building with numerous living units.*

were the women mentioned in innumerable tombstone inscriptions (see: *CIL* VI, 11602) exalting the domestic virtues of wives, mothers and mistresses of households who chastely passed their time spinning and weaving wool and directing slaves; and there were the outstanding examples of matronly fidelity among those who, like Arria Maggiore, were ready to share exile, death and suicide with their spouses: "When chaste Arria was offering to her Paetus that sword which with her own hand she had drawn from out her breast: 'If thou believest me', she said, 'the wound I have inflicted has no smart; but the wound thou shalt inflict – this for me, Paetus, has the smart'" (Martial, I, xiii). There were the perfect companions, good, clever, parsimonious, and yet great lovers of literature like Calpurnia, Pliny the Younger's third wife who, as he wrote, "sings my verses and sets them to her lyre, with no other master but Love, the best instructor" (*Ep.*, IV, xix); and there were others: The noble empress Plotina, Trajan's wife; the learned Helvia, Seneca's mother; Martia, daughter of Cremutius Cordus, who dared to publish her father's banned works after his death; and the list could be continued.

The diffusion of Christianity in the late Empire brought women back under male authority, for female 'fragility' (*fragilitas*) required a man's protection. The legal disqualification of women was evidenced by the presence of a lawyer (*advocatus*) at the side of wife and widow to look after her affairs. Socially, Christianity strenuously emphasized chastity, simplicity of dress, modesty and submissiveness. Just think of Tertullianus' writings (*Ad uxorem, De cultu foeminarum, De virginibus velandis*); think of the works of Saint Jerome (*De conservanda verginitate*, for example) which record of the growth of the ideal of a strict monastic life even among women. And think of *De nuptiis et concupiscentia*, and all of the passages in Saint Augustine's *Confessions* in which the "lust of the flesh" (*concupiscentia carnalis*) is singled out as the one true reason for man's estrangement from God.

Homes and Housing

The barbarian invasions completed the transformation. In Germanic law, the concept of *mundio*, the absolute power of the head of the household (later modified under the influence of Latin law to a simple principle of defense and legal assistance) subjugated women and deprived them of their freedom as they had never been subjugated and deprived since the founding of Rome.

The true Roman house, however, was not the isolated *domus* with an atrium and peristyle — the *domus* was the prerogative of only the wealthy few. The constantly increasing phenomenon of urban growth at the end of the Republic led to the division of the patrician *domus* into many rental apartments, and to the development of a vertical, multi-storied style of building designed to utilize urban space more efficiently. Real estate speculation entered the picture — investors even bought buildings and deliberately caused their partial collapse so that they could demolish and rebuild them to their liking (Strabo, V, 3, 7); and so did imperial laws limiting building heights. Six stories had been reached quickly; and the flimsy wooden framework supporting the top floor units meant a high percentage of risk for tenants: "But here we inhabit a city supported for the most part by slender props, for that is how the bailiff holds up the tottering house, patches up gaping cracks in the old wall, bidding the inmates to sleep at ease under a roof ready to tumble about their ears" (Juvenal, *Sat.* III, 193 ff.).

The *insula* was born. It was a huge, block-long, multi-unit apartment building, an all-masonry structure with an unplastered facing layer of brick. Along the street on the ground floor there were shops (*tabernae*), each with a back room and a mezzanine for the merchant's living quarters (see: *City Streets and Shops*, p. 48); on the courtyard were the more comfortable and elegant apartments. The innumerable three-to-five room living units on the upper stories had windows, and even galleries and balconies, built in wood or masonry. Apartment ceilings up to the second floor were made of masonry; above, they were of timber, with beams and lathing. The roofing

133. Relief model of an insula at Ostia. Rome, Museum of Roman Civilisation.

134. The entrance to the 'thermopolium' (inn) in the Via di Diana in Ostia.

# Cookery

Our acquaintance with Roman cooking is due, above all, to a recipe book named after Caelius Apicius, a famous gourmet of the Tiberian period; but in fact the book was rewritten many times between the 1st and 4th centuries A.D. The Apicius cookbook is divided into nine chapters (*libri*) which deal with sauces, chopped meats, greens, vegetables, poultry (including ostriches, cranes, peacocks, flamingos and parrots), quadrupeds, fish and a series of costly dishes some of which were absolutely prohibited by censorial anti-luxury laws. There are other recipes in Cato's *De re rustica*, in Columella's treatise by the same name and in the *Naturalis Historia* written by Pliny the Elder.

In addition to an overabundance of herbs and sharp spices, the omnipresent ingredient was *liquamen*, the liquid part of a pickle (*garum*) obtained as follows: "Place fish guts in a bowl and salt them: add anchovies, small mullets, picarels, sprats and every other sort of tiny fish, and salt them as well; set the fish in the sun so that the salt melts and the fish are marinated in the solution; and turn them often. When they are thoroughly sopped ... put them through a sieve ... The *garum* that has been sieved is called *liquamen*. The thick part that remains ... goes into a pickle called *alec*" (*Geoponica*, XX ad fin.; cf. Pliny, *N.H.* XXXI, 43).

Generally speaking, the taste of foods tended towards a hot, spicy, sweet-and-sour flavor; and pepper was used to season everything, even home-baked cookies (*dulcia domestica*): "Take seedless green dates or pitted ripe dates and fill them with walnuts or pine nuts and ground pepper; salt them on the outside; fry in hot honey and serve" (Apicius, VII, 11).

The more popular dishes had a meat base. The fact that the Romans frequently used game meats such as hare, venison, chamois, wild boar, crane, pheasant and partridge in addition to the poultry, mutton, beef, pork and their innards which are common today, indicated a different environmental situation: For Italy was rich in woodlands, and in vast uncultivated areas containing swamplands and ponds.

Methods for cooking meat varied from simple boiled or roast dishes to the popular stuffed meat platters of Rome. "Stuffed hare. Prepare the hare, dress it out and place it on a cutting board. Put into the mortar, pepper, ligusticum and oregano; bathe with *liquamen*; add cooked chicken livers, brains, lean meat cut into bits and three raw eggs; blend with *liquamen*. Stuff the hare and cover it with omentum [an abdominal membrane] and a sheet of papyrus paper; stick it on the spit and roast over a slow fire. Meanwhile, put more pepper and ligusticum in the mortar, crush, and bathe with *liquamen*; dilute with wine and *liquamen* and bring to a boil. When the mixture has come to a boil, bind with cornstarch and pour over the roast hare. Sprinkle with pepper and serve" (Apicius, VIII, 8).

In some of the more refined preparations, milk and honey were also used; and the tougher game birds were cooked *en croûte* to soften their meat and eliminate their gamey odor. "The bird will be tastier and more tender, and its fat will be preserved, if you coat it with a flour and oil mixture and then roast it" (Apicius, VI, 6).

Fish too (of both the salt and fresh water, and even *vivarium*-bred varieties) was a very widely-eaten food. There was greenfish and sprats for the table of common folk, and shell fish, mussels and expensive fancy fish for the board of the rich. Fish could be boiled, fried or roasted, but it was never served or eaten without a sauce. In Apicius' cookery book, two whole chapters, *libri IX* and *X*, were dedicated to fish sauces which, like the sauces for meats, were essentially composed of herbs, pepper, *liquamen*, oil, vinegar, wine and, frequently, honey. Here is a sauce for sprats: "Pepper, ligusticum, dry mint, cooked onion, honey, vinegar and oil. Pour over the sprats and sprinkle with chopped hard-boiled eggs" (Apicius, IX, 10).

But cooking at home was a rare phenomenon, except in the villas of the rich. Most people ate in the streets at irregular hours, just as the Asians do today. Taverns and street vendors offered the passersby roasted meat cubes, sausages, fried fish, sprats, olives, sweets, fruits and filled buns; like Martial's "pieman, who bawls as he carries round in his warm pans smoking sausages" (I, xli, 9 f.). Dinner was the main meal. It might consist of a modest supper among friends, with appetizers ("Sliced eggs shall garnish lizard-fish served with rue, and there shall be a paunch dripping from the tunny's brine", Martial, X, 48) and a single course (kid with beans and tender sprouts) as well as some of yesterday's leftovers; or it might be one of those glutton's spreads which were the target of wit-sharpened darts shot by Seneca, Petronius, Martial, Juvenal and, later, Macrobius, and for the after-effects of which one more sauce from Apicius' cookery book would seem appropriate: "Chop a five-finger's-worth pinch of cumin, half as much pepper and a peeled clove of garlic; bathe with *liquamen*; pour on a bit of oil a drop at a time. This sauce will relieve an upset stomach and facilitate digestion" (IX, 13).

I. *Fresco with a banquet scene. Rome, Catacomb of Saint Callixtus. The guests are seated on a 'sigma.'.*

II. *Relief with a banquet scene. Este, Archaeological Museum*

III. *Sarcophagus relief with a banquet scene. Rome, Museo delle Terme. Note the 'sigma' and the moulds for bread.*

IV. *Thermopolium (inn) sign with food and drink. Ostia, Via di Diana.*

V. *'Asaraton', a floor mosaic showing an illusionary unswept floor covered with banquet leftovers. Vatican, Gregorian Profane Museum.*

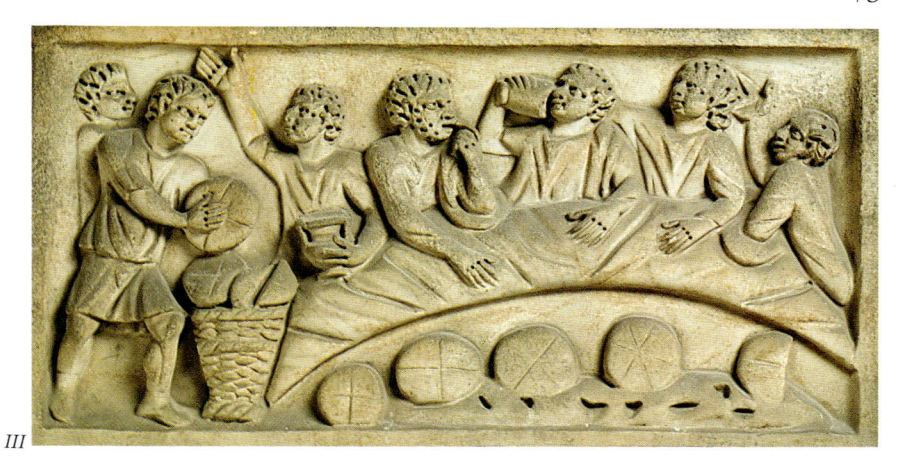

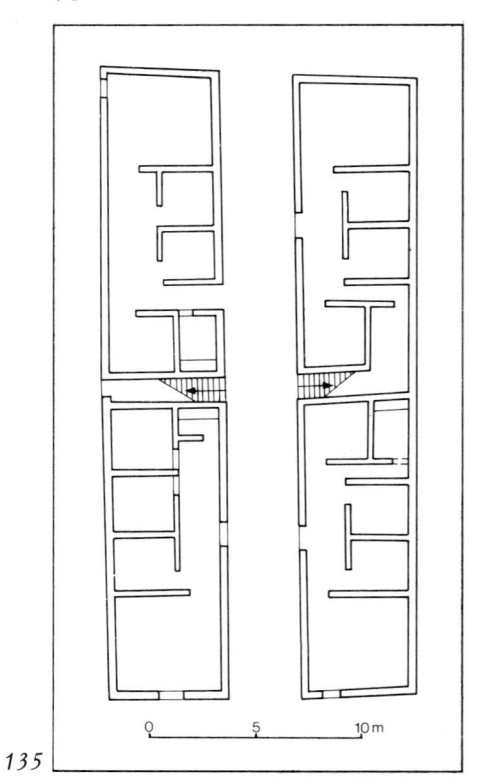

135. Plan of a typical detatched house in Ostia.

136. Palatine, House of Livia, fresco decorations of the 2nd style.

137. Plan of a large house with garden at Ostia.

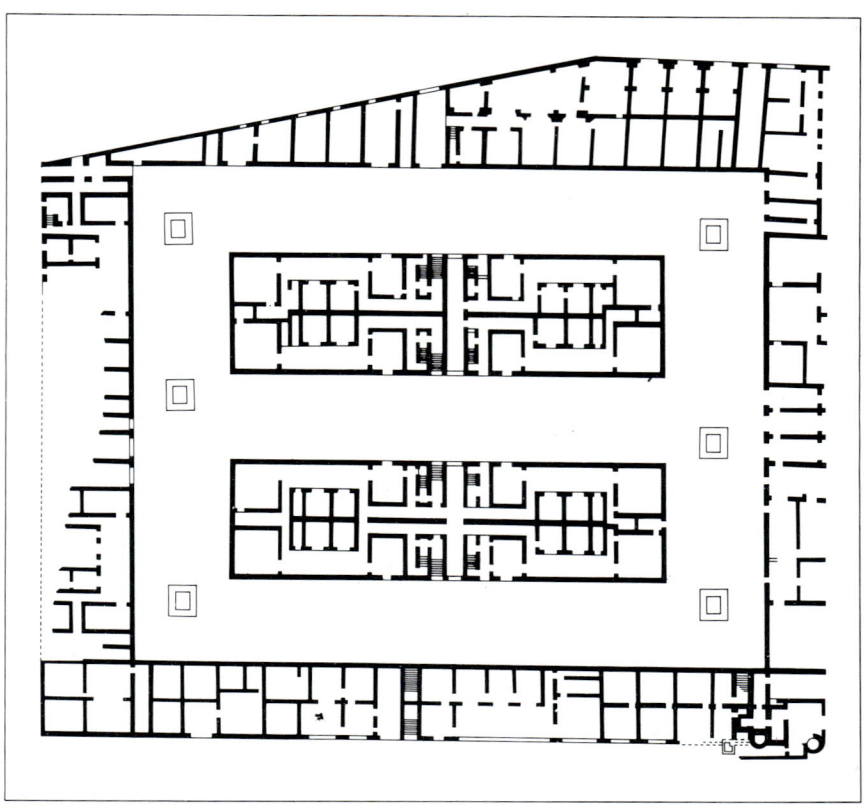

*138. The so-called Auditorium of Maecenas with 3rd-style paintings (end of the 1st century B.C.).*

was usually of flat and curved tiles. After Nero's fire, a portico was frequently built in front of the ground floor shops for protection.

The *insulae* have almost completely vanished from Rome — although one is still visible at the foot of the Aracoeli steps that was probably six stories high; but there is a vast collection of them at Ostia. Often a single apartment plan was repeated in a great array of apartments; or several living units were laid out around a central courtyard; or else, whole blocks of *insulae* were grouped into a complex surrounded by an open stretch of land containing gardens and fountains (these were the so-called 'Garden apartments'). Since the living units had absolutely no water or sanitary equipment, apartments in the large-scale *insulae* were furnished at the most with common facilities on the ground floor: A fountain, a bath, a toilet (*forica*) and frequently, among the *tabernae*, a dyer and cleaner's shop, the *fullonica*.

According to data in the Notitia Regionum Urbis XIV and other region listings of the period, at the beginning of the 4th century A.D. there were approximately 45,000 *insulae* in Rome, as against barely 1,800 one-family *domus*. The neighborhoods containing the worst crowding of poorer citizens into these rabbit hutches occurred above all in those located in the natural hollows between the hills and the Forum: Argiletum, with its numerous shoemaker's shops and bookstores; and ill-famed Subura, between the Esquiline and Quirinal Hills. The problem of a near-central location was a highly important one in an era when only the rich could afford a litter (*lectica*) for travel: "May I be shot but I should like, Decianus, to be with you all day and all night. But there are two miles that part us; these become four when I go and have to return. Often you are not at home; even although you are, often you are denied... Yet to see you I do not mind going the two miles; not to see you and to go four I do mind" (Martial, II, v).

# Mural Paintings

The only surviving pictorial works of ancient Rome are frescoes. There were once easel paintings, exhibited in temples and in other public buildings; and huge panels decorated with battle scenes, carried to the triumphal celebrations of the Roman generals. But the perishable materials did not permit them to endure.

Regarding fresco technique, we have Vitruvius' direct testimony: "When the cornices are finished, the walls are to be rough-cast as coarsely as possible [our present-day scratch-coat] ... A second and third coat is to be applied as the one underneath dries [these coats are composed of sand, pozzolana and lime]. When, in addition to the rough-cast, not less than three coats of sand have been laid, then coats of powdered marble are to be worked up, and the mortar is to be so mixed that when it is worked up it does not adhere to the trowel ... When a thick layer has been spread and is drying, a second thin coat is to be spread. And when this has been worked up and rubbed over, a still finer coat is to be applied [the three layers are made up of sand, powdered marble and lime]. When the walls have been made solid with three coats of sand and also of marble, they will not be subject to crack or any other fault ... When the colours are carefully laid upon the wet plaster, they do not fail but are permanently durable" (*De Arch.* VII, iii, 5,6,7).

Once the colours were dry, a varnish of Punic wax, slightly warmed and diluted with a little oil, was applied to protect them and made to penetrate the plaster by a wall-heating technique. Finally they were polished with clean linen cloths and waxed cord (Pliny, *N.H.* XXXIII, 40; Vitruvius, *De Arch.* VII, ix).

During the Empire, the layers enumerated by Vitruvius were reduced; and in the late period, only two were left — one scratch coat, and a single coat of plaster.

The oldest painting found in Rome is the fragment of a fresco decorating a tomb on the Esquiline Hill, and dating back to the early decades of the 3rd century B.C. Perhaps it represents episodes from the second Samnite War. This type of historical theme-painting soon made way for a style of decoration which derived from Hel-

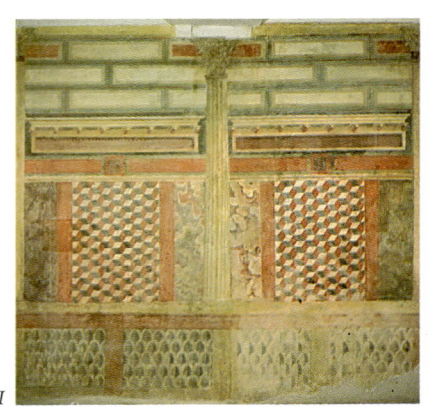

*I. Fragment of a fresco from a building on the Palatine. Rome, Antiquarium of the Palatine.*

*II. House of the Grifi on the Palatine, 2nd-style wall. Rome, Antiquarium of the Palatine.*

*III. House of Livia on the Palatine, room with late 2nd-style paintings. At the center of the wall are 'megalographiae' paintings.*

lenistic sources, and used perspective to break through the wall plane of the room and to expand and extend space. Here again Vitruvius, who wrote his treatise between 30 and 25 B.C., comes to our aid (*De Arch*. VII, v): "The ancients... began by imitating the variety and arrangement of marble inlay; then the varied distribution of festoons, ferns, coloured strips [the so-called 'first' style, used until about 80 B.C.]... Then they proceeded to imitate the contours of buildings, the outstanding projections of columns and gables [the first phase of the 'second' style, between 90 and 75 B.C.]; and in open places, like the exedrae, they designed scenery on a large scale in tragic, comic, or satyric style; in covered promenades, because of the length of the walls, they used for ornament the varieties of landscape gardening, finding subjects in... harbours, headlands, shores, rivers, springs, straits, temples, groves, hills, cattle, shepherds. In places, some have also the anatomy of statues [the high period of the 'second' style, which lasted until the end of the first century B.C.]... But these, which were imitations based upon reality, are now disdained... Instead of columns, there rise up stalks; instead of gables, striped panels with curled leaves and volutes. Candelabra uphold pictured shrines, and above the summits of these... [are] slender stalks with heads of men and of animals attached to half the body ['third' style, approximately 15 B.C. to 63 A.D.]".

From the year 35 until the end of the 1st century A.D., the tendency to use scenery and false architecture became even more accentuated, and actual theatrical settings were even painted in the panels, with figures moving freely about in them, like actors on a stage ('fourth' Pompeian style).

The practice of dividing the walls into three areas, with a larger central aediculum flanked by two smaller ones, was introduced with the second style and continued until the early decades of the 3rd century, although the architectural structures were increasingly reduced to a system of abstract red and green lines painted on a white ground. The heritage of 4th-style impressionistic-type painting survived in the small figures inserted in this abstract wall decoration; but the later artists, no longer culturally supported by Hellenistic naturalism, used its techniques to break down organic form and eliminate volume – to create symbols rather than to reproduce nature.

*IV. House of the Farnesina, late 2nd-style wall with typical three-compartmental wall decoration. Rome. Museo delle Terme.*

*V. Villa beneath the church of Saint Sebastian on the Appian Way, wall decoration dating from about 230-240 A.D. in which the three-compartmental scheme has survived.*

*139. Marble portal in the Domus of Protirus in Ostia.*

*140. Sallustian Gardens, ruins of a building of the 2nd century A.D.*

Nevertheless, proximity to the city center was an advantage paid for with discomfort, for it could not have been particularly pleasant to live in those ugly, dark and costly barrack-like buildings. "If you can tear yourself away from the games of the Circus, you can buy an excellent house at Sora, at Fabrateria or Frusino, for what you now pay in Rome to rent a dark garret for one year" (Juvenal, *Sat.* III, 223 ff.). And they were terribly noisy: "Beshrew me if I think anything more requisite than silence for a man who secludes himself in order to study! Imagine what a variety of noises reverberates about my ears! I have lodgings right over a bathing establishment. So picture to yourself the assortment of sounds, which are strong enough to make me hate my very powers of hearing! When your strenuous gentleman, for example, is exercising himself by flourishing leaden weights; when he is working hard, or else pretends to be working hard, I can hear him grunt; and whenever he releases his imprisoned breath, I can hear him panting in wheezy and high-pitched tones. Or perhaps I notice some lazy fellow, content with a cheap rubdown, and hear the crack of the pummeling hand on his shoulder, varying in sound as the hand is laid hollow or flat. Then, perhaps, a professional comes along, shouting out the score;

141. *House of the Farnesina, stucco decorations. Rome, Museo delle Terme.*

that is the finishing touch. Add to this the arresting of an occasional roysterer or pickpocket, the racket of the man who always likes to hear his own voice in the bathroom, or the enthusiast who plunges into the swimming-tank with unconscionable noise and splashing. Besides all those whose voices, if nothing else, are good, imagine the hair-plucker with his penetrating, shrill voice, for purposes of advertisement, continually giving it vent and never holding his tongue except when he is plucking the armpits and making his victim yell instead. Then the cakeseller with his varied cries, the sausageman, the confectioner, and all the vendors of food hawking their wares, each with his own distinctive intonation" (Seneca, *Ep. Mor.* LVI, 1 f.).

Things were no better at night. According to Juvenal, "most sick people here in Rome perish for want of sleep ... For what sleep is possible in a lodging? Who but the wealthy get sleep in Rome?" (*Sat.* III, 232 ff.). And even Martial complained: "Neither for thought, Sparsus, nor for quiet is there any place in the city for a poor man. Schoolmasters in the morning do not let you live; before daybreak, bakers; the hammers of the coppersmiths all day. On this side the money-changer idly rattles on his dirty table Nero coins; on that the hammerer of Spanish gold-dust beats his well-worn stone with burnished mallet; and Bellona's raving throng does not rest, nor the canting shipwrecked seaman with his swathed body, nor the Jew taught by his mother to beg, nor the bleary-eyed huckster of sulphur wares ... You, Sparsus, know nothing of these things, and cannot know ... you have country in the town ... and unfathomed depths of slumber and a stillness broken by no tongues, and no daylight unless you let it in. As for me, the laughter of the passing throng wakes me, and Rome is at my bed's head" (XII, lvii, 4 ff.).

*142. Villa of Livia at Prima Porta, 3rd-style frescoes with garden scenes. Rome, Museo delle Terme.*

The fortunate master Sparsus mentioned by Martial was not the only one to have "country in the town". In fact, in sharp contrast with the intensive housing of the populous districts stifled by their dearth of light, air and quiet, the homes of the few truly wealthy Romans had wide, open green surroundings to isolate them from the stir and bother of the city. Maecenas, the great patron of arts and letters, lived in a villa on the Esquiline to which Augustus retired when he sought to restore his failing health.

A large rectangular hall with an apse on Largo Leopardi, called the Auditorium of Maecenas, is all that survives of the villa buildings, which later became Imperial property. Painted in the hall's false windows were garden scenes.

Many other new villas sprang up in Rome. After 63 B.C., there stood on the Pincian Hill the famous terraced residence of Lucullus (level with today's Villa Medici) of which we have no more than a plan drawn by Pirro Ligorio and whose gardens were "counted among the most costly of the imperial gardens" (Plutarch, *Lucull.* XXXIX, 2). On the northern slopes of the Pincius were the villas of the Acilii, the Anicii and the Pincii: The Muro Torto is all that remains of their powerful substructures. Even the historian Sallust owned a villa (located in the area between today's Via Veneto and Via Salaria) which had vast gardens. It eventually became imperial property, and was later enhanced by Hadrian with structures similar to those he used to decorate his famous villa at Tivoli. Its impressive ruins may still be seen at the center of the present-day Piazza Sallustio.

Another villa, built between 30 and 25 B.C. and whose owner is unknown, rose on the right bank of the Tiber quite near to the Farnesina — hence its current name, House of the Farnesina. Several of its rooms, decorated with late 2nd-style paintings, have survived. The most remarkable of the murals, fluid chiaroscuro sketches of country or marine landscapes set against the whitewashed background of the rooms, call to mind Studius (or Ludius), that exceptional painter whom Pliny numbered among the few Roman artists worthy of remembrance: "Nor must Studius, also of the period of his late lamented Majesty Augustus, be cheated of his due, who first introduced the most attractive fashion of painting walls with pictures of country houses and porticoes and landscape gardens, groves, woods, hills, fish-ponds, canals, rivers, coasts, and whatever anybody could desire, together with various sketches of people going for a stroll or sailing in a boat or on land going to country houses riding on asses or in carriages, and also people fishing and fowling or hunting or even gathering the vintage" (*N.H.*, XXXV, xxxvii, 116).

The town villa had no fixed type. Each proprietor ordered architect's designs in accordance with his individual desires, often subordinating plans for the distribution of rooms in the *domus* to an appropriately scenic positioning of the buildings in their surrounding landscape, the grounds and the gardens – the *horti*. In fact, the *horti* were responsible for the name of the Roman town house, for the latin terms *villa* and *hortus*, in the singular, both indicated rustic and rural dwellings associated with agriculture. The distinction emerged when in the age of Sulla the new fashion of recreating country landscapes in the city took root and spread. Varro, in the Augustan era, notes that "The grandeur and pomp of the urban villa today is the main problem: Townsfolk compete with the country houses of Metellus and Lucullus: That they were ever built is a real public disaster" (*R.R.* I, xiii, 6-7).

A typical feature of these sumptuous town residences were the *horti* or gardens. The art of gardening (*opus topiarium*) suddenly arose towards the end of the 1st century B.C., and Pliny attributes the invention to a Roman, Gaius Matius (*N.H.* XII, 13). Gardens were divided up symmetrically by vertical and horizontal paths. At the center was a large square with a fountain. The paths were bordered with box-tree, rosemary and myrtle hedges, and herms, statues, vases and benches stood at the crossroads. Flower varieties were few; but the shrubs (especially the evergreens) were pruned with such great skill that they appeared in an infinite variety of geometrical shapes. The garden was often a *xystus*, a space enclosed by stonework porticoes, with a thick crisscrossing of overhanging tree boughs roofing over the paths; or else it was left seemingly wild, like the Persian *paradeisos* (paradise) adopted by the Greeks, and cultivated with a brilliant mixture of low, light and varied plants fenced in by reeds. For an idea of the Roman gardens one may turn to the beautiful wall paintings decorating a large marble paved hall in the suburban villa of Livia, on Via Flaminia just past Porta Prima – a villa once called "The White Hen Roost" (*ad gallinas albas*, Suetonius, *Galba*, I).

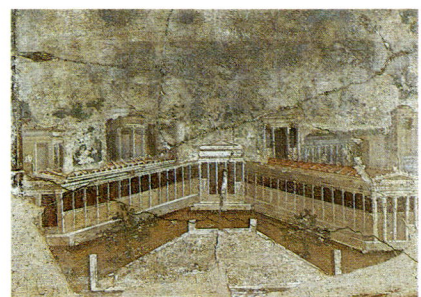

143. *Villa of Livia at Prima Porta, fresco detail. Rome, Museo delle Terme.*

144, 145. *Paintings showing an urban villa. Naples, National Archaeological Museum. The characteristic element is the portico which provided shade and cool and also allowed the inhabitants to walk outside when the weather was poor.*

## Hair Styles and Cosmetics

In the course of the centuries that separated Republican Rome from the Late Empire, the fashion in female hairdress changed many times over. What is more, during each period, there were hairstyles which differed according to one's age and social position; and for each single fashion, there were simple, everyday styles, and elaborate styles for important occasions.

During the Republican era, hairdos were simple. The head of hair, always divided by a parting down the center, was gathered in a bun at the nape of the neck or, in young people, in a pony tail; and occasionally the effect was softened by a fine fringe of curls resting on the forehead, or tiny braids encircling the face.

The comb, that indispensable tool, was made of bronze, ivory, bone, horn, tortoiseshell, and even of gold. It had a single row of teeth or, as was common in Imperial times, two rows, one with the teeth set close together, and one in which they were set farther apart. Some combs were also worn for ornament (Ovid, *Ars. Am.* III, 147; Pollux V, 96).

During the Augustan age, a central motif added a more elaborate touch to the Republican hairdo: A lock of hair was brushed forward in a wave decorating the center and then gathered into a tight braid; a bun at the back was composed of several braids entwined and wound together.

But not until the age of the Flavian Emperors and Trajan did female hairstyles acquire the richness and elaborateness that made them into monumental edifices of curls. "So numerous are the tiers and storeys piled one upon another on her head! In front, you would take her for an Andromache; she is not so tall behind: you would not think it was the same person", objects Juvenal in his famous satire of women (VI, 502 ff.).

In order to obtain lasting curls, the *calmistrum* (an iron heated over the incandescent coals) was used. It was hollow, in the shape of a rod — the very same curling iron that was still in use only two generations ago, before women began using the acids which produce permanents. To reinforce the finished product, there were hair-pins for clipping the hair in place and, of course, ribbons, nets, tiny combs, hairpieces (which were very voluminous in the latter part of the 4th century) and unguents to improve the resistence and consistency of one's hair. The hand of the hairdresser and the comber (whose male and female titles were *ornator, pectinator, ornatrix, pectinatrix*) was absolutely indispensible. In the homes of the rich, there was often a permanent post for the hairdresser.

Cosmetics also played an important role in the appearance of Roman women. Commerce in creams, perfumes and unguents flourished in each and every period of the city's life. The products were contained in small, fine ceramic vases, often elegantly decorated; or in glass phials; or in alabaster receptacles called *pissidi*; and they nearly always came from Greece or the Hellenistic East.

Makeup was diluted or mixed in small plates and saucers. The base was a lanoline, *oesypum*, made from the fat of unwashed sheep's wool, which also yields a salutary unguent. Lips and cheeks were tinted with red, obtained from ochre, from a lichen-like plant called *ficus*, or from mollusks. Black (soot or antimony powder) was used to outline the eyes and thicken the brows, which were very marked in nearly every period of Roman history. Finally, the temples were softened to a pale bluish shade, and the forehead whitened with gypsum or ceruse. Martial, Hamlet's forerunner, complains: "you lie stored away in a hundred caskets; and your face does not sleep with you — yet you wink with that eyebrow which has been brought out for you in the morning" (IX, xxxvii ff.).

The mirror was a basic necessity. A sheet of blown glass was laid over a sheet of metal, whether lead, bronze or a precious metal. The most handsome examples came from Alexandria, in Egypt.

I

II

III

*IV*

*V*

I. Bust of Julia Domna with Severian-age hairdo. Rome, Capitoline Museum.

II. Girl pouring perfumes. Rome, Museo delle Terme.

III. Long-necked glass balsam jars for perfumes and unguents. Aquileia, Archaeological Museum.

IV. Tomb stele of Via Statilia. Rome, Palace of the Conservators. Detail of the head of the deceased. The hairdo is that of a middle-class married woman of the mid-1st century B.C.

V. Portrait of a married woman from the Tomb of the Haterii. Vatican, Gregorian Profane Museum. The heavily waved styling of the hair was in vogue among the middle classes around 100 A.D.

VI. Female portrait from El Faiyum. Florence, Archaeological Museum. Note the very carefully prepared makeup.

*VI*

*146, 147. Above, portrait of Tiberius; below, that of Nero. Florence, the Uffizi.*

*148. Plan of the Palatine.*
1. *Lupercal*
2. *Ancient huts*
3. *Stairway of Cacus*
4. *Temple of the Magna Mater*
5. *House of Augustus*
6. *Temple of Apollo*
7. *House of Livia*
8. *Cryptoporticus*
9. *Basilica*
10. *Aula Regia*
11. *Lararium*
12. *Peristyle*
13. *Nymphaeum*
14. *Triclinium*
15. *Peristyle*
16. *Courtyard*
17. *Stadium*
18. *Domus Praeconum*
19. *Paedagogium*
20. *Circus Maximus*

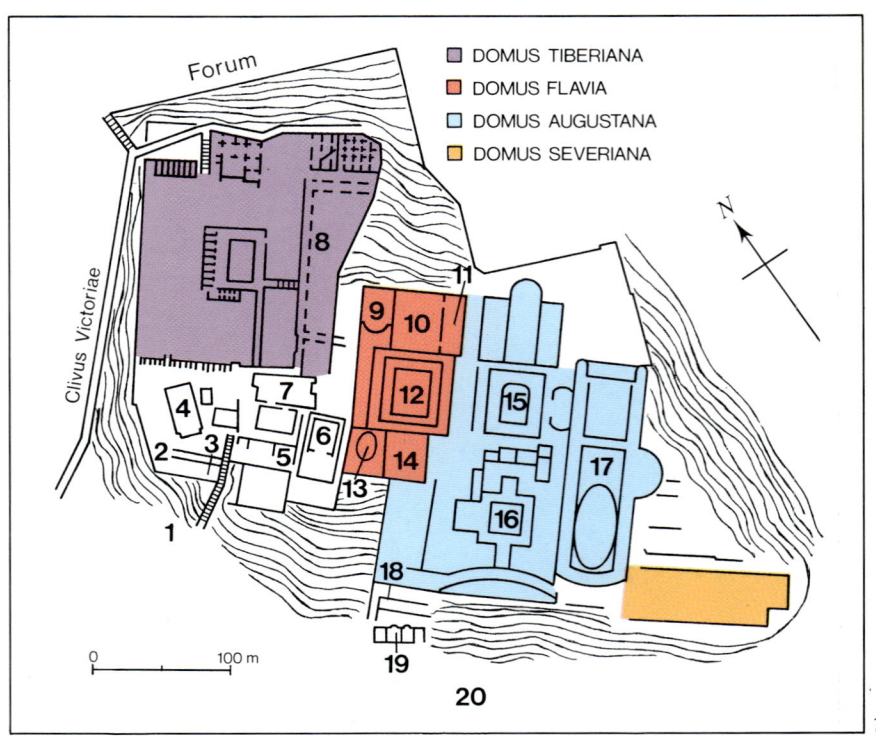

## The Imperial Palace

The basic atrium and peristyle plan of the *domus*, enhanced by all the comforts, luxuries and natural beauties typical of the town villa, had its most impressive development in the imperial residences on the Palatine, named 'palaces' after *Palatium*, the name of the hill.

The first imperial *domus* was the Domus Tiberiana, built by Tiberius on the western corner of the hill. Its remains were earthed over in the 16th century by the Farnese Gardens, and very little is visible now. Nevertheless, we know that it was built around an enormous peristyle at the center of today's garden area.

After the terrible fire of 64 A.D., Nero had a field day in Rome: "There was nothing however in which he was more ruinously prodigal than in building. He made a palace extending all the way from the Palatine to the Esquiline, which at first he called the House of Passage [Domus Transitoria], but when it was burned shortly after its completion and rebuilt, the Golden House [Domus Aurea]. Its size and splendour will be sufficiently indicated by the following details: Its vestibule was large enough to contain a colossal statue of the Emperor a hundred and twenty feet high; and it was so extensive that it had a triple colonnade a mile long. There was a pond too, like a sea, surrounded with buildings to represent cities beside tracts of country, varied by tilled fields, vineyards, pastures and woods, with great numbers of wild and domestic animals.... When the edifice was finished in this style and he dedicated it, he deigned to say nothing more in the way of approval than that he was at last beginning to be housed like a human being" (Suetonius, *Nero*, XXXI, 1-2; cf. Tacitus, *Ann*. XV, 42).

The remains of a splendid polychrome marble pavement belonging to the Domus Transitoria can be seen beneath the Domitian-age pavement in the nymphaeum to the right of the Coenatio Iovis in the Domus Flavia. Another structure probably belonging to the Domus Transitoria is the cryptoporticus situated alongside the Domus Tiberiana and decorated with ceiling stuccoes (the originals, now at the Antiquarium, are replaced by copies). Also on display at the Antiquarium of the Palatine is the decorated vault of a nymphaeum.

The enormous complex of buildings called the Domus Aurea ("one large house then occupied all of Rome" writes Martial, *Ep*. II, 4) had the plan of a

# The Imperial Palace

149. Palatine, the Domus Tiberiana viewed from the Forum Romanum.

150. Fragment of the pavement of the Domus Tiberiana. Rome, Antiquarium of the Palatine.

151. Palatine, the ascent of the Clivus Victoriae beneath the impressive arcades of the Domus Tiberiana.

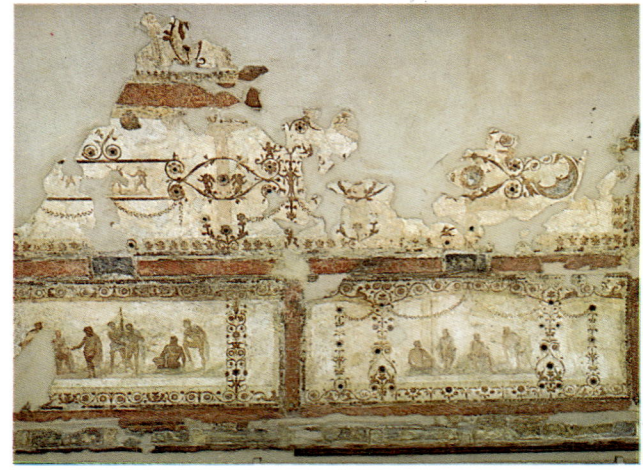

152. *Palatine, cryptoporticus of the Domus Transitoria, stucco decorations. Rome, Antiquarium of the Palatine.*

153. *Palatine, Domus Transitoria, frescoes of a nymphaeum ceiling vault. Rome, Antiquarium of the Palatine.*

154. *Domus Aurea, octagonal hall.*

villa, and spread across an area lying between the Palatine, the Velian Ridge and the Caelian Hill and including the entire valley of the Colosseum, where Nero excavated his artificial lake. The only portion of the structure to survive today lies on the Oppian Hill, below Trajan's baths, for whose decoration Nero's palaces were stripped of marbles, columns and precious objects. In the rooms of the west wing there are wall paintings, examples of the 3rd style; their author is usually given the name of another of the famous Roman painters commemorated by Pliny: "Another recent painter was Fabullus (or Famulus), a dignified and severe but also very florid artist; to him belonged a Minerva who faced the spectator at whatever angle she was looked at. Famulus used to spend only a few hours a day in painting, and also took his work very seriously, as he always wore a toga, even when in the midst of his easels. The Domus Aurea (Golden House) was the prison that contained his productions, and this is why other examples of his work are not extant to any considerable degree" (*N.H.* XXXV, xxxvii, 121).

When the Renaissance painters visited the Domus Aurea's underground rooms, which they called 'grottoes', they drew inspiration from the decoration containing slim, fantastical plant forms with slender miniature human and ani-

# The Imperial Palace

155. Palatine, Domus Flavia, the peristyle.

156. Palatine, Domus Flavia, the western nymphaeum of the 'Coenatio Iovis'.

157. Palatine, Domus Flavia, pavement of the triclinium known as the 'Coenatio Iovis'.

158. Palatine, Domus Augustana, nymphaeum of the west wing, level with the lower peristyle.

mal figures and phantom architecture with an aerial perspective, and they named these painted ornaments, appropriately, 'grotesques'.

The more heavy handed, typically 4th-style paintings in the east wing, on the other hand, have led critics to attribute this portion of the pavilion to a later imperial residence, that of Titus (Domus Titi).

But the imperial palace par excellence, even in the eyes of the ancients, was Domitian's residence, built at the end of the 1st century A.D. by the great architect Rabirius and covering the whole central portion of the Palatine Hill. It consisted of state apartments, the Domus Flavia, and residential palace buildings, the Domus Augustana, as well as recreational areas containing the stadium and the baths.

The Domus Flavia was a complex of halls of peerless magnificence. Behind a colonnaded podium standing about 10 meters above a facing esplanade called the Area Palatina was the Throne Room (Aula Regia), from whose apse Domitian, "master and god" (*dominus et deus*; see: *The Divine Majesty of the Emperor*, p. 90), made his public appearances. Surrounding the Aula Regia were niches containing variously coloured marble statues (now in the Museum of Parma), entablatures

# The Divine Majesty of the Emperor

On January 16th, 27 B.C., the Senate decreed that the title '*Augustus*' be conferred upon Octavius. It was an entirely new title, differing substantially from those conferred on his predecessors (Sulla was named *Felix*, Pompey entitled *Magnus*). The difference, according to the historian Dio Cassius (LIII, 16, 8), lay in the fact that *Augustus* signified "that he was more than human".

But Octavius never used *Augustus* as a title, he simply adopted it as his name; and in the *Res Gestae*, a history of his works that he himself wrote, he selected '*princeps*', which meant the 'first' among free citizens, to designate his position. In fact, if at the end of the 6th century A.D. Gregory the Great could write: "Herein lies the difference between the Kings of barbarian nations and Emperors of the Roman State: Barbarian Kings are the masters of slaves, whereas Roman Emperors rule free men" (*Ep.* XI, 4). There can be no doubt that the concept of the free citizen, founded upon the authority of law, must never have deserted the Roman mind.

Nevertheless a slow deification of the person and the family of the Emperor began with the principate.

Augustus was the first to introduce the cult of the emperor's *genius*. Every man had a *genius* or *numen*, which was his divine part – or, rather, the life-force of his family. To worship the *genius* of the *princeps*, therefore, was a fairly discreet sort of homage, consonant with the Roman mentality and acceptable to the citizen's mind.

Afterwards, more explicit steps toward deification were taken. Suetonius tells of Caligula: "And he came near assuming a crown and changing the principate into a monarchy. But on being reminded that he had risen above the elevation both of princes and kings, he began from that time on to lay claim to divine majesty; for after giving orders that such statues of the Gods as were especially famous for their sanctity or their artistic merit, including that of Jupiter of Olympia [the chryselephantine statue of Zeus by Phidias], should be brought from Greece in order to remove their heads and put his own in their place, he built out a part of the Palace as far as the Forum, and making the temple of Castor and Pollux its vestibule, he often took his place among the divine brethren, and exhibited himself there to be worshipped by those who presented themselves" (Calig. XXII, 1-3).

Claudius must have been no less exacting, for Suetonius writes that Lucius Vitellius (the future emperor) "first began to worship Gaius Caesar [Claudius] as a god; for on his return from Syria he did not presume to approach the emperor except with veiled head, turning himself about and then prostrating himself"; what is more, "he begged of Messalina [the Empress] as the highest possible favor that she would allow him to take off her shoes; and when he had taken off her right slipper, he constantly carried it about between his toga and his tunic, and sometimes kissed it" (*Vitell.* II, 5).

Nero had a colossal statue of himself, portrayed as Helios, the Sun God, placed in the immense vestibule of the Golden House; and he appeared in the great circular banquet hall of his Palace, "which revolved day and night, like the heavens" (Suetonius, *Nero*, XXXI, 2), as the father of the Cosmos (*kosmokrator*, an iconography which lasted until the early Christian and Medieval representations of Christ) – that is, as the source of its movement.

Domitian adopted an even more explicit position: "With no less arrogance he began as follows in dictating a circular letter in the name of his procurators, 'Our Master [*dominus*] and Our God [*deus*] bids that this be done'. And so the custom arose of henceforth addressing him in no other way in writing or in conversation" (Suetonius, *Domitian* XIII, 2).

Commodus identified himself with Hercules and had the Senate pass a resolution "giving him the name Hercules and calling him a god" (*Script. Hist. Aug. Comm.* VIII, 9). But the "divine majesty" of the emperor was not publicly accepted until the beginning of the 3rd century; with the advent of the Severi, the members of the imperial family were worshipped in a divine cult, not, as previously, after their death and apotheosis, but while they were still among the living.

From that time on, the Emperors increasingly adopted the ceremonials, attributes and symbols of the gods, until finally the Constantinian concept of imperial power as divine right appeared and investiture, which still derived from the Roman people in Ulpian's law texts, was completely forgotten: "...myself, to whose care [God almighty] with His heavenly sanction entrusted the government of all earthly things" (Octatus, *App.* III in *CSEL* XXVI).

*I. Hadrian-age tondo on the Arch of Constantine. The head of Constantine, which supplants Hadrian's head, is encircled by the 'nimbus' or halo. Herodian writes of Commodus as well that "it is said that a heavenly glow hovered about his head" (I, 7, 5). The nimbus was adopted by Christian iconography for God and the saints.*

*II. Base of the 'Magistri Vici'. Vatican, Gregorian Profane Museum. Base of an altar or sculptural group which depicts a sacrificial procession. The togaed personages to the left are neighborhood or 'vicus' magistrates ('magistri vici'), functionaries of the cult of the Lares and the 'genius' of the emperor. The latter are represented in statuettes in the hands of the bare-foot figures shown in front of the magistrates.*

*III. Statue of the Emperor Claudius in the guise of Jove. Vatican, Pio-Clementine Museum.*

*IV. Bust of Commodus in the guise of Hercules. Rome, Capitoline Museum.*

91

II

III

IV

V. Arch of the Moneychangers. Relief with Septimius Severus and Julia Domna. The Empress is shown with the crescent, considered a divine attribute, on her head, and raising her right hand in the gesture of power and blessing which spread through Rome together with the oriental deity cults. The gesture – as well as its meaning – was to have a long life in Christian iconography.

VI. Detail from the base of Antoninus' Column showing the apotheosis of Antoninus Pius and his wife Faustina. Vatican Museums. A winged genius guides the couple through the skies.

*159. Palatine, Domus Augustana, room serving as passageway, with niches on a level with the upper peristyle.*

*160. Palatine, Domus Augustana, the lower peristyle with a fountain basin showing a motif of four 'peltae' (Amazon shields).*

*161. Palatine, Domus Flavia, the marble decoration of the nymphaeum pavement.*

*162. Palatine, Domus Augustana, the so-called Stadium.*

and marble inlays, and a coffered wooden ceiling extending over a full 30 meters.

To one side of the Throne Room was the council hall or *auditorium*, commonly called the Basilica, and to the other what was probably a waiting room or a room where the emperor's guard was stationed, the so-called Lararium.

All of these halls, which could also be reached through a branch of Nero's cryptoporticus, opened to the south into an immense peristyle with Numidian marble columns, nyphaea to each side, and a labyrinthine fountain in the center.

On the south side of the peristyle was another huge chamber, the imperial *triclinium*. Cool in summer, with windows looking out on two lateral nymphaea containing huge fountains; warm in winter, with hot-air heating under a pavement of polychrome marble: This was the fabulous 'Banquet of Jove', the *Coenatio Iovis*. Behind the glorious banquet hall, another colonnade led to two chambers each with an apse: They were probably libraries.

The Domus Augustana, the private residence of the emperor whose north wing may also have been designed for purposes of state reception, resembled a villa more closely in structure. The last buildings contained a two-storied succession of alternating exedrae, nymphaea and pool basins with aediculae, extending as far as the final great exedra with its glorious view over the Circus Maximus.

The villa plan was equally apparent in the stadium area, which served not only as private hippodrome but also as Palace Gardens or *Viridarium*; it was evi-

The Imperial Palace

dent too in the *thermae* area, later rebuilt by Maxentius.

On the south corner of the Palatine, Septimius Severus erected the last of the great imperial *domus*, the Domus Severiana, whose magnificent artificially terraced brickwork arcades (the structures on which the palace once stood) are still visible today.

Ruins do survive, however, on the slopes overlooking the Circus Maximus. They belonged to the servants' quarters, and were the so-called Paedagogium, a school for imperial slaves and, to the south, the Domus Praeconum (the House of the Heralds) with Severus-age paintings and floor mosaics which are now on display at the Antiquarium of the Palatine.

As long as Rome was the capital of the Empire, imperial Caesars ruled the world from the *domus* which Domitian had built and Severus enlarged – from the 'palace' par excellence. A barbarian, Theodoric, was the last tenant. Even today, the palace's marvels can be easily imagined from the magnificence of its ruins, the beauty of its surviving marble pavements, the sad glory of its fragments: Cornices, capitals, sculpted entablatures lying abandoned on the grass; and especially for the sweeping views it commanded, from the valley of the Circus Maximus to the Aventine and Caelian Hills, to the reddish mass of Caracalla's *thermae*, to the tomb of Caecilia Metella on the Appian Way and far, far off in the distance, to the gentle swells and undulations of the Alban Hills spread out against the horizon.

*163. Palatine, Domus Severiana, the powerful arcades of the palace substructure.*

*164. Palatine, Paedagogium, detail of the decoration of the architrave.*

*165. Palatine, Domus Praeconum, Severian age frescoes. Rome, Antiquarium of the Palatine.*

*166. Palatine, view from the south. To the left are the ruins of the Domus Augustana; to the right, the arcades of the Domus Severiana.*

*167. Portrait of Domitian. Rome, Capitoline Museum.*

# Index of Names

Accius (2nd century B.C.) 53
Alexander Severus (emp. 222-235 A.D.) 42
Ancus Marcius (king 7th century B.C.) 5
Antoninus Pius (emp. 138-161 A.D.) 9, 91
Apicius (1st century A.D.) 74, 75
Augustine (Saint 354-430) 32, 55, 58, 60, 72
Augustus (emp. 23 B.C. - 14 A.D.) 6, 7, 10, 18, 20, 22, 24, 26, 27, 29, 34, 40-42, 44, 51, 60, 65, 66, 71, 82, 83, 90
Aurelianus (emp. 270-275 A.D.) 10, 42

Barsanufius (6th century A.D.) 55

Caesar (emp. 100-44 B.C.) 7, 15, 18, 19, 22, 24, 37, 42, 53, 56
Caligula (emp. 34-41 A.D.) 90
Caracalla (emp. 211-217 A.D.) 55, 59, 62, 90, 93
Cassiodorus (480-575 A.D.) 20
Cato (1st century B.C.) 74
Catullus (87-54 B.C.) 36, 49, 55, 71
Cicero (106-43 B.C.) 19, 26, 31, 37, 51, 65, 70, 71
Cincius Alimentus (3rd century B.C.) 3
Claudius (emp. 41-54 A.D.) 26, 41, 42, 90
Columella (1st century A.D.) 74
Commodus (emp. 180-193 A.D.) 90
Constantine (emp. 306-337 A.D.) 10, 15, 26, 31, 34, 40, 63, 90

Dio Cassius (155-235 A.D.) 40, 90
Diocletian (emp. 284-305 A.D.) 10, 19, 60, 62, 63
Domitian (emp. 81-96 A.D.) 20, 28, 40, 49, 50, 53, 86, 89, 90, 93

Elagabalus (emp. 218-222 A.D.) 52
Ennius (239-168 B.C.) 53, 57
Eunapius (345-420 A.D.) 32

Fabius Pictor (260-200 B.C.) 3

Galba (emp. 68-69 A.D.) 27
Galen (129-201 A.D.) 63
Gregory the Great (Saint 537-604 A.D.) 90

Hadrian (emp. 117-138 A.D.) 9, 15, 25, 30, 36, 56, 60, 82
Hellanicus of Mytilene (5th century B.C.) 3
Horace (68-8 B.C.) 32, 52, 58

Jerome (Saint 347-420 A.D.) 55, 60, 72
Juvenal (60-135 A.D.) 36, 37, 44, 48, 51, 52, 55, 58, 60, 63, 68, 71, 73, 75, 77, 81, 84

Livy (59 B.C. - 17. A.D.) 3
Lucan (39-65 A.D.) 6

Marcus Aurelius (emp. 161-180 A.D.) 9, 36, 60
Martial (40-104 A.D.) 44, 49, 51, 55, 68, 70, 72, 75, 77, 81, 84, 88
Maxentius (emp. 306-312 A.D.) 10, 26, 31, 36, 93

Naevius (3rd century B.C.) 53, 57
Nero (emp. 54-68 A.D.) 9, 26, 29, 40, 45, 47, 59, 73, 86, 88, 90
Nerva (emp. 96-98 A.D.) 9, 28

Octatus (4th century A.D.) 90
Olympiodorus (5th century A.D.) 41
Ovid (43 B.C.-17 A.D.) 5, 56, 84

Pacuvius (3rd-2nd century B.C.) 53, 57
Persius (34-62 A.D.) 40, 55, 60
Petronius (?-66A.D.) 71, 75
Phaedrus (1st century A.D.) 31
Phocas (emp. 602-610 A.D.) 9, 10
Plautus (254-184 B.C.) 12, 13, 29, 53, 57
Pliny the Elder (23-79 A.D.) 6, 53, 56, 74, 78, 82, 83, 88
Pliny the Younger (62-114 A.D.) 31, 49, 68, 72
Plutarch (46-120 A.D.) 17, 82
Pollux (2nd century A.D.) 84
Procopius (6th century A.D.) 42, 44, 90

Romulus 3, 11, 24, 37

Sallust (86-35 B.C.) 82
Scipio (235-183 B.C.) 16, 54
Seneca (4 B.C.-65 A.D.) 54, 59, 72, 75, 81
Septimius Severus (emp. 193-211 A.D.) 10, 13, 28, 30, 34, 42, 90, 93
Socrates (380-440 A.D.) 55
Statius (45-96 A.D.) 68
Strabo (63 B.C.-19 A.D.) 7, 73
Suetonius (70-140 A.D.) 9, 20, 22, 24, 65, 66, 83, 86, 90
Sulla (138-78 B.C.) 18, 83, 90

Tacitus (54-120 A.D.) 3, 9, 26, 51, 53, 86
Tarquinius Priscus (King, 4th century B.C.) 11
Terence (185-159 B.C.) 53, 57
Tertullianus (160-250 A.D.) 72
Tiberius (emp. 14-37 A.D.) 15, 20, 24, 26, 31, 86
Timaeus (346-250 B.C.) 3
Titus (emp. 76-81 A.D.) 25, 30, 51, 62, 89
Trajan (emp. 98-117 A.D.) 9, 28, 30, 34, 40-42, 56, 72, 84, 88

Valentinian I (emp. 364-375 A.D.) 60
Valentinian II (emp. 383-392 A.D.) 10
Valentinian III (emp. 419-455 A.D.) 52
Varro (116-27 B.C.) 3, 64, 83
Vespasian (emp. 69-79 A.D.) 25, 26, 60
Virgil (70-19 B.C.) 32, 56
Vitellius (emp. 69 A.D.) 26, 90
Vitruvius (1st century B.C.) 58, 64, 67, 70, 78, 79

# Index of Places

Aqua Appia 6, 43
Aqua Marcia 43, 63
Aqueduct of Alexander Severus 42
Aqueduct of Claudius 43
Aqueduct of Trajan 42
Amphitheatre of Caesar 45
Amphitheatre Castrensis 52
Amphitheatre of Curio 45
Amphitheatre of Statilius Taurus 46
Ara Pacis 24, 30
Arch of Constantine 36, 90
Arch of Septimius Severus 9, 10, 21, 25, 30, 36

Arch of Titus 9, 10, 25, 30
Arce 11
Argiletum 11, 19, 77
Auditorium of Maecenas 15, 77, 82
Aula Isiaca 66
Aula Regia 89
Aurelian Walls 9, 10, 15, 20, 53

Base of the Decennalia 35
Basilica Aemilia 12, 17
Basilica Argentaria 60
Basilica Iulia 9, 10, 19, 22, 25, 34
Basilica of Maxentius 10, 36
Basilica Opimia 12
Basilica Porcia 12
Basilica Sempronia 12, 19

Baths of Caracalla 55, 59, 62, 90, 93
Baths of Constantine 62
Baths of Diocletian 10, 62, 63
Baths of Ostia Antica 62
Baths of Titus 9, 62
Baths of Trajan 58, 62, 88

Caelian Hills 9, 11, 63, 88, 93
Campus Martius 6, 7, 9, 10, 16, 24, 30, 46, 53, 56, 59
Capitoline Hills 4-7, 10-12, 29
Castra Misenantium 47
Castra Praetoria 26
Cavern of Cacus 5
Circus of Caligula 45
Circus Flaminius 45
Circus of Maxentius 10, 15, 39, 45
Circus Maximus 6, 37, 41, 92, 93
Cispius 11
Clivus Argentarius 48
Clivus Victoriae 87
Cloaca Massima 5, 6, 11
Colosseum 3, 9, 40, 44-47, 51-53, 56, 88
Column of Antoninus Pius 27
Column of Phocas 9
Column of Trajan 21, 28, 29, 34
Comitium 11, 12, 17, 19
Curiae Veteres 4
Curia Hostilia 11, 17, 19
Curia Iulia 17, 19, 22, 30

Domus Augustana 89, 92, 93
Domus Aurea 47, 86, 88, 90
Domus of Cupid and Psyche 64
Domus Flavia 5, 86, 89
Domus Praeconum 93
Domus Protiri 80
Domus Severiana 93
Domus Tiberiana 86, 87
Domus Titi 89
Domus Transitoria 86, 88

Esquiline 11, 77, 78, 82, 86

Fagutal 11
Ficus Ruminalis 11, 34

Forum Augusti 24, 25, 29
Forum Boarium 3, 5, 32
Forum Caesaris 23, 25, 55, 60
Forum Holitorium 4, 5
Forum Nervae 32
Forum Pacis 10
Forum Romanum 2, 4, 5, 7, 10-12, 17-19, 22, 29, 34, 35, 45, 66, 70, 77, 90
Forum Traiani 29, 34, 60

Horti Agrippinae 45
Horti Sallustiani 80
House of Augustus 66, 70
House of the Farnesina 79, 82
House of the Grifi 15, 65, 78
House of Livia 15, 66, 67, 76, 78
House of the Vestal Virgins 11, 13, 32

Insula of the Charioteers 72
Iuturnae fountain 5, 11

Lacus Curtius 11, 13
Lapis Niger 11
Ludus Magnus 41, 46
Ludus Matutinus 44
Lupercal Cave 5

Mausoleum of Augustus 6, 7, 15
Mausoleum of Hadrian 15
Mercati Traianei 15, 48
Murcia Valley 41

Oppian Hills 11, 62, 88

Paedagogium 32, 93
Palatine Hills 3-7, 9-11, 14-16, 37, 41, 43, 64, 65, 70, 86-90, 93
Pantheon 7, 21, 29
Pincian Hills 82
Plutei Traiani 34
Pons Aemilius 6
Pons Fabricius 6
Pons Milvius 6, 36
Pons Sublicius 6
Porta Ardeatina 9
Porta Latina 9
Porticus Aemilia 15
Porticus Deorum Consentium 19

Quirinal 11, 29, 63, 65, 77

Regia 11, 14
Ripa Marmorata 21
Roma Quadrata 3, 65, 66
Rostra 9, 11, 22

Servian Walls 5, 6, 14, 15
Shrine of Venus Cloacina 11, 12
Stadium of Domitian 50, 53
Subura 24, 77

Tabernae Veteres 13, 19
Tabularium 9, 16-18

Tarpeian Rock 11
Temple of Antoninus and Faustina 5, 25, 31
Temple of Apollo 6, 16, 65, 66
Temple of Apollo Sosianus 25, 52, 56
Temple of the Capitoline Triad - (Jupiter, Juno, Minerva) 6,11, 14
Temple of Ceres 6
Temple of Concordia 9, 17, 18, 24, 25
Temple of the Dioscuri (Castor and Pollux) 6, 10, 11, 24, 25, 34, 90
Temple of Divus Iulius 5, 22, 34
Temple of Divus Vespasianus 9, 25
Temple of Faunus 16
Temple of Hercules Victor 4
Temple of Ianus 11
Temple of Iuno Regina 16
Temple of Iupiter Status 16
Temple of Largo Argentina 6, 42
Temple of Magna Mater 5, 15, 16, 32, 65
Temple of Mars Ultor 24
Temple of Peace 25
Temple of Portunus 32
Temple of Saturn 6, 9, 11, 16
Temple of Venus Cloacina 12
Temple of Venus Genetrix 19, 25
Temple of Venus and Rome 15, 25, 31
Temple of Vesta 11, 13
Templum Divi Traiani 29
Tiber Island 6, 16, 17
Tomb of Caecilia Metella 93
Tomb of Eurysaces 42
Tomb of the Haterii 84
Tomb of Romulus 15
Theatre of Balbus 56
Theatre of Marcellus 7, 52, 56
Theatre of Ostia Antica 53
Theatre of Pompey 53

Velian Ridge 25
Via Appia 10, 15, 79, 93
Via Biberatica 48
Via Sacra 5, 12, 30
Via Salaria 5, 82
Via Statilia 85
Via Tiburtina 26
Vicus Tuscus 13, 34
Villa of Livia 82, 83
Villa Publica 6
Viminal 11

# Contents

Introduction:
The Urban Development of Rome, 3

## Political Monuments, 11

Building Techniques, 14
Monument Maintenance, 20
Law and Order, 26
Religion and Superstition, 32

## Public Buildings, 37

Supplies, 42
City Streets and Shops, 48
Personal Hygiene, 54
Education, 60

## Homes and Housing, 64

Home Furnishings, 68
Cookery, 74
Mural Paintings, 78
Hair Styles and Cosmetics, 84

## The Imperial Palace, 86

The Divine Majesty of the Emperor, 90

Index of Names, 94
Index of Places, 94